CAIRO

TRAVEL GUIDE

2025

Discover Ancient Wonders, Modern Marvels, and Timeless Traditions in the Heart of Egypt's Iconic Capital

MAP OF CAIRO

TO VIEW THE MAP, SCAN THE CODE.

TABLE OF CONTENTS

INTRODUCTION

Cairo. The name alone conjures up thoughts of ancient treasures, a large city teeming with activity, and an alluring blend of past and modern. My voyage to this iconic destination began with a long-simmering curiosity: I wanted to encounter not only the enormous pyramids or the legendary Nile but also the heartbeat of a city that has thrived for millennia.

Cairo welcomed me with a tumultuous, exuberant embrace from the time I arrived. The air was heavy with history, with the aroma of spices from bustling marketplaces, the murmur of Arabic conversations, and the odd call to prayer ringing from adjacent mosques. It was unlike anything I'd ever experienced both overwhelming and exhilarating. Cairo was more than just a tourist destination; it was a metropolis meant to be felt, tasted, and understood.

I recall walking into Tahrir Square for the first time, its energy pulsing with layers of stories that have shaped not only Egypt but the entire world. My gaze was pulled to the high Cairo Tower, a lighthouse dominating the city as if keeping watch over the myriad stories beneath. This was a location where the antique and modern merged seamlessly. Every area seemed to contain a secret waiting to be discovered.

What struck me the most, however, were the people. Their warmth and openness reflected the vibrancy of the city itself. Whether it was a vendor selling falafel on a quiet street or a young artist enthusiastically describing her work at a museum nestled away in Zamalek, each interaction felt personal, as if Cairo had planned it specifically for me.

Of course, the allure of the pyramids was strong. Standing on the edge of Giza, starring at these enormous monuments to human achievement, I was astounded. What resonated with me was not simply their majesty, but the way the villagers spoke about them—with pride, as if the pyramids were family members whose stories they had inherited. This link, this profound sense of belonging, gave Cairo its spirit.

Wandering through Khan El Khalili bazaar was another eye-opener. The colors, sounds, and fragrances were all enticing a kaleidoscope of gold jewelry, complex textiles, and the pleasant aroma of freshly made mint tea. It was more than just a market; it was a living museum of Cairo's culture. And, as my backpack got heavier with trinkets and treasures, I couldn't resist the want to keep exploring and absorbing.

Cairo isn't a city that can be easily summarized. It demands your attention, challenges you to dig deeper, and rewards you with memories that will last long after you leave. It's the kind of location that lingers in the back of your mind, calling you back when you least expect it. Even today, as I reflect on my first moments in Cairo, I understand that it was more than simply a destination; it was an experience that redefined what it means to genuinely explore a city.

WHY CAIRO IS THE BEATING HEART OF EGYPT

Cairo is Egypt's dynamic heartbeat, a metropolis that seamlessly combines the ancient and modern. As the capital and largest city, it's a location where history echoes around every corner and the vitality of daily life beats with an irrefutable tempo. Cairo's rich culture, traditions, and experiences frequently capture visitors.

The city has profound origins dating back to the Pharaoh era, and its streets depict the story of civilizations that created the world. Walking through Cairo is like going through a living museum.

The magnificent Great Pyramids of Giza and the enigmatic Sphinx are everlasting emblems of creativity and determination. Beyond these world-famous buildings, the Egyptian Museum has a treasure trove of treasures, including Tutankhamun's golden mask and numerous relics that reveal the mysteries of the past.

Cairo, however, is more than just a historical site. The city is thriving and strikes a mix between modernization and tradition. The skyline is accented by modern skyscrapers, yet vibrant bazaars like Khan El Khalili transport you to another period with their vivid displays of spices, textiles, and handcrafted items. The noises of bartering merchants and the smells of freshly brewed mint tea create a sensory experience that will stay with you long after you leave.

Life beside the Nile River enhances the city's charm. The river, which has sustained Egypt for millennia, remains a lifeline for the city. Traditional feluccas cruise by luxury riverboats and the reflection of city lights on the water makes a stunning view, especially when the sun sets. Dining aboard a boat or simply wandering along the Corniche allows you to fully experience Cairo's relationship to this historic river.

Religion also has an important role in defining Cairo's identity. The city is home to amazing mosques, such as the Mosque of Muhammad Ali, which sits atop the Citadel and offers panoramic views of the city below. Nearby, the historic streets of Coptic Cairo are home to historical churches and sites that reflect the city's unique spiritual past. This coexistence of faiths reflects Cairo's diverse ethnicities and cultures.

The city's culinary environment is a voyage in its own right. The cuisine scene is both traditional and interesting, with street sellers selling koshari, a nourishing blend of rice, lentils, and pasta, and high-end restaurants providing polished versions of Egyptian staples. Every meal is an adventure with freshly made bread, flavorful stews, an abundance of dates, and desserts such as basbousa.

What makes Cairo genuinely unique is its people. They exemplify the city's essence, being warm, hospitable, and full of stories. Conversations with locals can provide insight into life in this ever-changing metropolis, highlighting nuances that guidebooks frequently overlook.

Cairo's dynamic vitality is unparalleled, and it makes a lasting impression on those who visit. The city is more than just a place; it's an experience, a tale, and a link to something far more than the present instant. Walking its streets reveals why Cairo is Egypt's pulsing heart, a location where the past and future combine uniquely.

A GLIMPSE OF THE CITY'S STORIED PAST AND THRIVING PRESENT

Historic Foundations

Cairo's story originates on the Nile River, where civilization was founded thousands of years ago. The Giza Plateau, which includes the renowned pyramids and the enigmatic Sphinx, exemplifies ancient architects' creativity. Walking these sites gives you a sense of kinship to the pharaohs who presided over one of history's most powerful civilizations.

The Egyptian Museum, located near Tahrir Square, displays a remarkable collection of artifacts. Its treasures, like Tutankhamun's golden mask and ancient papyrus scrolls, shed light on Egypt's cultural and creative achievements. Exploring the museum is like peeling back the layers of a civilization that had a tremendous impact on the world.

Cultural Richness

Cairo's streets are vibrant and colorful, reflecting the various influences that have influenced its character throughout the years. Islamic Cairo, a UNESCO World Heritage site, is a tangle of small streets and historical mosques. The Al-Azhar Mosque, with its centuries-old minarets, remains a beacon of knowledge and devotion. Nearby, the Khan el-Khalili bazaar is bustling with activity, with traders selling everything from handcrafted jewelry to scented spices.

A walk through this neighborhood provides an experience with the traditions that characterize Cairo's spirit. Whether seeing artisans at work or sipping a cup of strong Egyptian coffee in a centuries-old café, the atmosphere creates a unique experience.

Modern flourishes

While its past is prominent, Cairo's modern side is also captivating. The city's skyline is punctuated by high-rises and modern structures, providing a peek at its ambitious future. The Cairo Tower, which stands tall on Gezira Island, offers panoramic views of the sprawling metropolis. In contrast, Zamalek, a green area on the same island, offers a more tranquil side of city life, complete with art galleries, boutique stores, and diverse restaurants.

The Grand Egyptian Museum, which is set to be one of the world's largest archeological museums, exemplifies the seamless integration of the past and contemporary. Designed to conserve and display Egypt's rich past, this cutting-edge facility will quickly become a must-see for visitors.

The pulse of daily life

Cairo's attractiveness stems from its contrasts. The call to prayer reverberates throughout the city, mixing with the sounds of bustling traffic. Feluccas float along the Nile, their sails catching the breeze, while riverbank promenades fill with families enjoying the evening air. Local restaurants feature dishes of koshari and falafel, reflecting the city's culinary traditions.

Cairo's inhabitants are its heartbeat. Their warmth and endurance give the city a sense of vibrancy. Whether they're negotiating in the marketplaces, sharing stories over a meal, or simply going about their business, they exemplify the spirit of a place that has survived and prospered for millennia.

CHAPTER 1

1. ESSENTIAL PLANNING FOR CAIRO

WHEN TO VISIT: SEASONS, WEATHER, AND FESTIVALS

Seasons and Weather

Winter (December to February):

This period is often considered the most comfortable for exploring Cairo. Daytime temperatures hover between 60°F and 70°F, providing pleasant conditions for sightseeing. The evenings can get chilly, so layering your clothing is advisable. Winter is a peak tourist season, with visitors flocking to marvel at the Pyramids of Giza, the Sphinx, and the treasures of the Egyptian Museum without the sweltering heat.

Spring (March to May):

Spring in Cairo brings mild temperatures, typically ranging from the mid-60s to the upper 80s°F. The days are warm without being overwhelming, making it an excellent time to explore outdoor attractions like Al-Azhar Park or take a felucca ride along the Nile. However, occasional dust storms, known as the "khamsin," may disrupt plans, so staying updated on weather conditions is wise.

Summer (June to August):

The summer months are the hottest in Cairo, with daytime temperatures often exceeding 95°F. Although the heat can be intense, it's also the period when fewer tourists visit, which means shorter lines at popular attractions. Early mornings and evenings are the best times to venture outdoors, while afternoons are ideal for indoor experiences like museum visits or exploring historic mosques.

Autumn (September to November):

Autumn is another pleasant season for exploring Cairo. Temperatures begin to cool, dropping to the 70s and 80s°F, and the city's gardens and parks offer a refreshing escape. The lower tourist density during this time provides a more relaxed atmosphere for exploring bustling bazaars or taking a stroll through Islamic Cairo's historic streets.

Festivals and Cultural Highlights

Cairo's rich cultural calendar adds another layer of excitement to your visit. Celebrations and festivals bring the city to life, offering visitors a glimpse into its vibrant traditions.

Ramadan and Eid Celebrations:

During Ramadan, the Islamic holy month, Cairo takes on a unique rhythm. While daylight hours may feel quieter, the city transforms after sunset with vibrant evening markets and gatherings. Following Ramadan, the festivities of Eid al-Fitr feature joyous feasts and family celebrations, adding a lively touch to the city.

Cairo International Film Festival (November):

International filmmakers and moviegoers flock to this esteemed occasion. Screenings and cultural events held during the festival offer creative insight into both Egyptian and international cinema.

Pharaonic Festival (February):

Held annually, this celebration honors Egypt's ancient heritage with parades, music, and performances inspired by the grandeur of the pharaohs. It's a captivating way to immerse yourself in the country's historical roots.

Sphinx Festival (Dates Vary):

Focusing on traditional Egyptian arts and spirituality, this festival features workshops, performances, and interactive sessions. It's an excellent opportunity to connect with local culture and history.

GETTING THERE AND AROUND: FLIGHTS, PUBLIC TRANSPORT, AND TAXIS

Cairo International Airport (CAI), located 14 miles northeast of the city center, serves as the main airport for both local and international travelers. Airlines like EgyptAir, Emirates, and Lufthansa provide regular flights at cheap prices depending on the season and booking time. For example, direct flights from New York to Cairo normally cost between $700 and $1,200 in economy class, although regional connections from nearby locations such as Amman or Dubai might cost as little as $200.

The airport has three main terminals that are connected by a free shuttle service, allowing for easy transfers. When travelers arrive, they can take pre-arranged hotel shuttles, airport taxis, or ride-hailing apps to their rooms. Local taxis frequently charge between 250 and 400 EGP (about $8 to $13) to central Cairo, depending on traffic. For those looking for a more convenient experience, Uber and Careem provide dependable options with upfront pricing and air-conditioned automobiles, which typically cost between 150 and 300 EGP.

Public Transportation: An Affordable Exploration

Cairo's metro system is one of the most efficient and cost-effective methods to get about the city. With three operational lines spanning key areas, the metro provides a speedy alternative to congested roadways. Tickets cost as little as 5 to 10 EGP, depending on the distance, and trains run from 5 a.m. until midnight. Tahrir Square (Sadat Station), the Giza Pyramids (Al Ahram Station on the new Line 4), and Maadi, a famous residential suburb, are also major stops.

Public buses and minibusses travel throughout the city, connecting places not served by the metro. While incredibly inexpensive, with rates starting at 3 EGP, these options can be congested and difficult for non-Arabic speakers. Tourists may prefer modern, air-conditioned buses operated by firms such as Go Bus, which also offers routes to sites beyond Cairo, including Alexandria and Sharm El Sheikh. Tickets for these intercity buses run between 150 and 350 EGP, depending on the route and type of service.

Taxis and ride-hailing services: comfort right at your fingertips.

Taxis are still a viable option for short travel, with white and yellow cabs available throughout the city. White cabs use meters but make sure the driver turns them on before starting your journey. Short journeys are normally priced between 20 and 50 EGP, depending on traffic and distance. Yellow taxis can be pre-booked using apps or phone calls for more peace of mind and comfort, with fixed rates and greater service standards.

Ride-hailing services are quite popular in Cairo due to their ease of use and fair pricing. Apps like Uber and Careem dominate the industry, with fares determined by distance and demand. Trips inside inner neighborhoods often cost between 50 and 150 EGP, whereas journeys to outside districts may cost slightly more. These apps also accept credit cards, which adds another layer of ease.

Private car rentals are offered from Sixt and Avis. Daily prices for a compact automobile start at about 500 EGP, excluding gasoline. Drivers must have an international driving permit and be prepared for Cairo's unpredictable traffic conditions.

Insider Tips for a Smooth Experience.

1. Currency Issues: Always carry small denominations of Egyptian pounds, as taxi drivers and bus conductors may not have changed for larger notes.

2. Avoid Rush Hours. Peak traffic congestion occurs in the morning (8-10 a.m.) and evening (5-8 p.m.). If possible, schedule outings at off-peak hours to save time on transport.

3. Stay Connected: Before heading overseas, download maps and translation applications to help you navigate and overcome language hurdles.

WHERE TO STAY:

LUXURY HOTELS

1. Four Seasons Hotel Cairo at Nile Plaza

Located in the heart of the city, this five-star property offers breathtaking views of the Nile River and is a prime spot for exploring Cairo's historic landmarks. The rooms are elegantly designed with spacious interiors, luxurious bedding, and marble bathrooms. Guests can enjoy a variety of gourmet dining options, including Italian, Chinese, and Middle Eastern cuisines.

Price Range: Starting at $400 per night for a standard room; suites can go up to $1,500.

Location: Corniche El Nil, Garden City.

Tips: Request a Nile-view room for stunning sunsets. Early booking is recommended, especially during peak tourist seasons.

2. The St. Regis Cairo

This towering masterpiece along the Nile blends traditional Egyptian artistry with contemporary design. The hotel features lavishly appointed rooms, an opulent spa, and a rooftop pool offering panoramic city views. Dining options include diverse international cuisines, curated by world-class chefs.

Price Range: Rooms start at $350 per night, with premium suites exceeding $1,800.

Location: Corniche El Nile, Downtown Cairo.

Tips: Don't miss the signature butler service, which adds a personalized touch to your stay.

3. Kempinski Nile Hotel Cairo

This boutique hotel is renowned for its cozy yet luxurious ambiance. Located along the Nile, it offers chic accommodations, complete with private balconies, rain showers, and handcrafted amenities. Guests can unwind at the rooftop pool or dine at the Blue restaurant, known for its exquisite Mediterranean dishes.

Price Range: Rates begin at $250 per night; suites start at $800.

Location: Corniche El Nil, Garden City.

Tips: Take advantage of the free nightly chocolate hour— a delightful experience for anyone with a sweet tooth.

4. Fairmont Nile City

Situated within the Nile City Towers, this property exudes modern sophistication. The hotel offers a range of rooms with river views, an infinity pool, and a lively rooftop bar. Its central location makes it ideal for both business and leisure travelers.

Price Range: Standard rooms are available from $220 per night, while luxury suites cost upwards of $1,000.

Location: Corniche El Nile, Ramlet Beaulac.

Tips: Visit the rooftop during the evening for some of the best cityscape views in Cairo.

5. Sofitel Cairo Nile El Gezirah

This French-inspired luxury hotel sits on the southern tip of Gezira Island, providing a serene escape amidst the city's energy. Its spacious rooms and suites are adorned with contemporary décor, and guests can enjoy a riverside dining experience at the in-house restaurants.

Price Range: Rooms start at $200 per night; suites can go up to $900.

Location: El Gezirah Street, Zamalek.

Tips: Book a table at the riverside restaurant for a memorable dining experience with a view.

BUDGET-FRIENDLY

1. City View Hotel

Price: Approximately $40–$60 per night

Location: 1 El Bostan Street, Tahrir Square

Description: Overlooking the iconic Egyptian Museum, this property offers spacious rooms with comfortable furnishings and modern amenities. Guests can enjoy free Wi-Fi, 24-hour room service, and a rooftop restaurant serving both local and international dishes. Its proximity to Tahrir Square makes it a convenient base for exploring the city.

Tips: Ask for a room with a view of the museum for an added treat, especially at night when the museum is beautifully lit.

2. Osiris Hotel

Price: Approximately $30–$50 per night

Location: 49 Nobar Street, Bab El Louk

Description: This family-run boutique hotel is known for its warm hospitality and charming atmosphere. The rooftop terrace provides sweeping views of Cairo's skyline, making it a peaceful spot to unwind after a day of sightseeing. Rooms are simply furnished yet clean and cozy, offering everything needed for a restful stay.

Tips: Opt for breakfast on the terrace—it's a delightful way to start your day with fresh local flavors and a panoramic view.

3. Dahab Hostel

Price: Approximately $10–$20 per night

Location: 26 Mahmoud Bassiouny Street

Description: Perfect for budget-conscious travelers, this laid-back option is popular among backpackers and solo adventurers. The property features shared and private rooms, along with a communal rooftop area that fosters a friendly, social vibe. Its central location makes it easy to access key landmarks and bustling markets.

Tips: Book well in advance, as this hostel is often fully occupied during peak travel seasons.

4. Talisman Hotel

Price: Approximately $50–$80 per night

Location: 39 Talaat Harb Street, Downtown

Description: Combining affordability with a touch of old-world charm, this boutique hotel offers uniquely decorated rooms that reflect Egyptian art and history. Guests appreciate its quiet ambiance, despite being located in the heart of the city. Complimentary breakfast and attentive service add to its appeal.

Tips: Explore the nearby cafes and bookshops that give the area a distinct character.

5. Guardian Guest House

Price: Approximately $40–$70 per night

Location: 1 Abou Al Hool Street, Nazlet El Samman

Description: Located just steps away from the Great Pyramids of Giza, this property boasts unparalleled views of these ancient wonders. Rooms are simple yet comfortable, and the rooftop terrace offers a front-row seat to the nightly sound-and-light show at the pyramids. The welcoming staff and individualized care are frequently praised by visitors.

Tips: Request a room facing the pyramids for a unique and unforgettable experience.

WHAT TO PACK: ESSENTIALS FOR COMFORT IN THE DESERT CITY

Clothing for the Climate

Cairo's weather is typically hot and dry, so lightweight, breathable fabrics are important. Opt for cotton or linen shirts, loose-fitting pants, and skirts to keep cool during the day.

Long-sleeved tops and pants are recommended to protect your skin from the sun and to respect local norms. A wide-brimmed hat or scarf is a must-have to shield your face and neck from the sun's intensity, while sunglasses with UV protection will keep your eyes safe in the bright light.

Comfortable walking shoes are vital, as many sites involve walking on uneven terrain or sandy paths.

Sun Protection and Hydration

The sun in Cairo can be fierce, so bring a high-SPF sunscreen to avoid sunburn, and remember to reapply throughout the day. A refillable water bottle is highly suggested, especially one with an insulated design to keep your drink cool. Staying hydrated is important, as the heat can be dehydrating even if you don't feel thirsty. Electrolyte packets can also be helpful to restore minerals lost during the day.

Practical Accessories

A lightweight daypack is handy for bringing your essentials, such as water, snacks, and a guidebook. A small, portable first-aid kit with bandages, antiseptic wipes, and any personal medicines is always a smart addition. Don't forget a universal power adapter to keep your gadgets charged, as Egypt uses a different plug system. A travel lock can provide added security for your belongings, especially in crowded places.

Cultural Considerations

Respect for local practices is important. A lightweight scarf or shawl can serve multiple purposes, including covering your shoulders when viewing religious sites. Carrying some cash in small amounts is useful for tipping and smaller purchases, as many places don't accept credit cards.

Tech and Gadgets

For capturing the city's stunning sites and bustling streets, pack a reliable camera or smartphone with ample storage. A power bank is a lifesaver to keep your gadgets charged throughout the day. If you plan on keeping connected, consider a local SIM card or an international data plan.

Personal Comfort

Pack a travel-sized hand cleaner, as public restrooms may not always have soap. Wet wipes are another great option to keep fresh throughout the day. Lightweight travel clothes that can layer easily will also prepare you for any evening temperature drops, especially during winter months.

Optional Items

Binoculars can enhance your experience at historical sites by giving a closer view of intricate carvings and details. A small notebook or diary is ideal for jotting down your thoughts or sketching memorable moments.

CULTURAL ETIQUETTE: DO'S AND DON'TS FOR TRAVELERS

Respecting Local Dress Codes

Cairo is a blend of modernity and tradition, and this balance is reflected in its expectations for clothing. While the city is relatively cosmopolitan, modest attire is appreciated, especially when visiting religious sites such as mosques. Lightweight, loose-fitting clothing that covers the shoulders and knees is ideal, not just for cultural sensitivity but also for comfort in the warm climate.

Women may also consider carrying a scarf for entering mosques, as covering the head is often required.

Greetings and Politeness

Greeting someone properly in Cairo demonstrates respect. A warm smile and a simple "Salam Alaikum" (peace be upon you) are well-received. Shaking hands is common, though men should wait for women to initiate the gesture. Politeness and patience go a long way in conversations. Egyptians value hospitality, and even a brief encounter can turn into an invitation for tea or coffee. Graciously accepting or politely declining with thanks is appreciated.

Dining Etiquette

Food is central to Egyptian culture, and sharing a meal is an experience that often fosters connections. If invited to someone's home, it's customary to bring a small gift, such as sweets or flowers, as a token of gratitude. When dining, it's polite to wait until your host begins eating before you do. Using your right hand for eating, passing dishes, and accepting items is customary, as the left hand is considered less clean in traditional contexts.

Photography Awareness

Cairo's beauty is captivating, but photographing people, particularly women, requires sensitivity. Always get someone's consent before taking their picture. In some religious or traditional settings, photography may be unwelcome, so observe signs or inquire politely. Capturing the grandeur of monuments and streetscapes is usually allowed, but respecting personal boundaries ensures a more respectful interaction.

Navigating Taxis and Public Transportation

When using taxis or other forms of transport, negotiate fares upfront to avoid misunderstandings. Ride-hailing apps are widely available and provide a straightforward option for getting around. Public transportation can be an adventure, but it's important to remain aware of personal space and avoid crowded areas during peak times.

Interactions in Markets and Shops

Cairo's markets are lively and full of character. It's popular to bargain, particularly in areas like Khan El Khalili Bazaar. Approach it with good humor, as it's seen as part of the shopping experience. While negotiating, maintain politeness and avoid being overly assertive. Vendors are accustomed to tourists and usually appreciate respectful interaction.

Understanding Religion and Prayer Times

Islam is a significant part of daily life in Cairo, and the city's rhythms often align with prayer times. You'll hear the call to prayer echoing from mosques throughout the day. While visitors don't need to participate, being mindful of these moments and avoiding loud conversations near mosques is considerate. Fridays are particularly important as they are the main day of worship.

General Courtesies

Patience is key in Cairo, where the pace of life can sometimes feel chaotic. Traffic, crowds, and bustling marketplaces are part of the city's charm, but they can be overwhelming. Staying calm and polite in all interactions helps you adapt to the flow of the city. Remember, a genuine smile and a kind word often leave a lasting impression.

CHAPTER 2

2. EXPLORING ANCIENT CAIRO

GIZA PYRAMIDS AND THE SPHINX: EGYPT'S MOST ICONIC LANDMARKS

The Magnificence of Ancient Architecture

The Pyramids of Giza, built during Egypt's Fourth Dynasty over 4,500 years ago, were created as monumental tombs for pharaohs. The biggest and most famous, the Great Pyramid, is credited to Pharaoh Khufu and was originally covered in smooth white casing stones that reflected sunlight. Nearby, the smaller pyramids of Khafre and Menkaure add to the grandeur of this historical site.

Equally interesting is the enormous limestone statue known as the Great Sphinx, which has the head of a man and the body of a lion. Standing guard near the pyramids, it's thought to represent Pharaoh Khafre and represents strength and wisdom. Over time, its enigmatic expression has inspired countless myths and theories, leaving visitors in awe of its historical and artistic importance.

Entrance Fees and Tickets

To explore the Pyramids and Sphinx, visitors need to purchase entry tickets, which can vary based on the type of access. General admission passes to the Giza Plateau cost approximately 240 Egyptian Pounds (EGP) for adults and 120 EGP for students. For a closer look inside the Great Pyramid, additional tickets are needed and cost about 440 EGP for adults and 220 EGP for students. Tickets for the smaller pyramids are more affordable, often running from 100 to 150 EGP.

To save time, consider buying tickets online or coming early to avoid long queues, especially during peak tourist seasons. Many travelers recommend opting for guided tours, as they often include entry fees, transportation, and the knowledge of an Egyptologist, making the experience more informative and convenient.

Tips for a Smooth Visit

1. Timing Matters: Arrive early in the morning to enjoy cooler temps and fewer crowds. Sunrise is particularly serene, giving great opportunities for photos.

2. Stay Hydrated: The desert heat can be intense, so take water and wear sun-protective clothing. Hats and sunscreen are also important.

3. Comfortable Shoes: Exploring the vast Giza Plateau involves a lot of walking, so comfortable footwear is a must.

4. Respect the Site: Avoid climbing on the pyramids or touching the Sphinx, as these practices are banned to preserve the monuments for future generations.

5. Camera Rules: Photography is allowed on the plateau, but using tripods or drones often needs special permits.

Getting There

The Pyramids of Giza are easily reachable from Cairo. A taxi or ride-hailing service is a popular choice, with costs averaging 100–150 EGP from downtown Cairo. Public buses and the Metro are more budget-friendly but can be less handy. Many hotels also offer private trips with transportation included.

Enhancing the Experience

Visiting the pyramids at night for the Sound and Light Show is a unique way to enjoy their grandeur. The show uses lighting effects and narration to tell the story of ancient Egypt, bringing the monuments to life in a different way. Tickets for this experience usually range from 300 to 350 EGP, and it's best to book in advance.

SAQQARA AND THE STEP PYRAMID: THE CRADLE OF PYRAMID BUILDING

Designed by the renowned architect Imhotep for Pharaoh Djoser, the Step Pyramid is acknowledged as the earliest large-scale stone edifice in human history. Before this innovation, Egyptian rulers were buried beneath flat, rectangular structures known as mastabas.

Imhotep's vision converted these into a sequence of piled terraces, constructing a pyramid that soared above the desert sands. This pioneering design became the prelude to the more famous smooth-sided pyramids at Giza, making Saqqara a crucial milestone in Egypt's architectural history.

As you approach the site, the sheer magnitude of the Step Pyramid is awe-inspiring. Built over 4,600 years ago, its limestone slabs have endured the test of time, weathering both natural elements and human activities. The pyramid's six-tiered form reflects a combination of practicality and spiritual symbolism, depicting the pharaoh's climb to join the gods in the afterlife.

Surrounding the Step Pyramid is a complex that once comprised ceremonial halls, courtyards, and temples. One of the most fascinating aspects is the entrance portico, a majestic passageway lined with columns that give a sense of timeless grandeur. Walking among these relics, it's impossible not to sense the weight of history that saturates the air.

Saqqara is home to an array of tombs embellished with beautiful carvings and vivid portrayals of daily life in ancient Egypt. These photos offer a rare view into the culture, economy, and beliefs of a society that lived millennia ago. The craftsmanship in these tombs is remarkable, depicting scenes of agriculture, feasts, and religious rituals, all carefully preserved under layers of sand until their discovery.

Another noteworthy component of Saqqara is the Serapeum, a complex of underground galleries that served as the ultimate resting place for sacred Apis bulls. These massive granite sarcophagi highlight the incredible skill of ancient builders, leaving modern visitors stunned by their accuracy and magnitude.

Visiting this place is not simply a journey into Egypt's past but a reflection of humanity's continuous ambition to create and invent. Saqqara encapsulates the ambition and vision of a society that sought to honor its kings and gods in ways that continue to enchant the world.

DAHSHUR'S RED AND BENT PYRAMIDS: LESSER-KNOWN MARVELS

The Red Pyramid: A Glimpse of Innovation

The Red Pyramid, attributed to Pharaoh Sneferu of the Fourth Dynasty, is often considered the first successful attempt at constructing a true smooth-sided pyramid. Its reddish hue, caused by the oxidized limestone used in its construction, gives the structure its name. One of Egypt's greatest pyramids, it rises to an astonishing height of around 344 feet.

What sets this monument apart is its architectural stability. Unlike earlier attempts, it showcases the perfected technique that later enabled the construction of the Great Pyramid at Giza. Visitors can explore its interior, where narrow passageways lead to a series of chambers, each revealing the ingenuity of ancient engineers. Standing in its shadow, one cannot help but admire the sheer determination and skill that went into its construction.

The Bent Pyramid: A Unique Masterpiece

A short distance from the Red Pyramid lies the Bent Pyramid, another creation of Pharaoh Sneferu. This structure is famous for its unusual shape, with its lower section rising at a steeper angle before abruptly shifting to a shallower slope. This distinctive design is believed to have resulted from an attempt to avoid structural collapse during construction.

The Bent Pyramid offers a rare opportunity to see two original entrances—one on the northern side and another on the western side. Its limestone casing remains remarkably intact, providing a rare view of how these monuments originally appeared. The pyramid's unique design reflects an important experimental phase in

Egyptian architecture, making it a must-visit site for anyone interested in history.

Practical Information for Visitors

1. Entry Fees: As of now, the general entrance fee to the Dahshur archaeological site is approximately 80 EGP (around $3) for international visitors. Additional charges may apply if you wish to enter the pyramids themselves, typically ranging between 50 and 100 EGP ($2–$4).

2. Getting There: Dahshur is about 40 kilometers south of Cairo and can be reached by car or taxi. To improve your experience, think about hiring an experienced guide.

3. Timing: The site is generally open daily from early morning until sunset. Arriving early is recommended to avoid crowds and make the most of your visit.

EGYPTIAN MUSEUM: A TREASURE TROVE OF ANTIQUITIES

Highlights of the Collection

The museum is home to an amazing array of treasures, numbering over 120,000 artifacts. Visitors are often drawn to the displays dedicated to the legendary Tutankhamun. The famed golden mask of the boy king is a standout piece, celebrated for its craftsmanship and historical importance. Equally remarkable are the jewelry, chariots, and funerary objects found in his tomb, which offer a glimpse into the life and beliefs of ancient Egyptian royalty.

Other famous exhibits include the royal mummies, statues, and papyri, each with its own story to tell. The museum's collection spans thousands of years, from the Predynastic Period to the Greco-Roman era. Each room is carefully curated, showing an in-depth narrative of ancient life, spirituality, and artistry.

Practical Information

The Egyptian Museum is open daily, and ticket prices are available to a range of visitors. General admission usually costs around 200 Egyptian pounds for adults and 100 pounds for students. Children under six can often enter for free. For those wishing to view the royal mummies collection, an additional fee of approximately 180 pounds is needed. Prices may vary slightly, so it's wise to confirm at the ticket counter or through official resources before going.

Tips for a Memorable Visit

To make the most of your time, try arriving early in the day. The museum can become quite busy, especially during peak tourist seasons. Hiring a knowledgeable guide is recommended for a richer experience, as they can provide background and insights that bring the artifacts to life. Alternatively, audio guides are usually offered at the entrance.

Photography policies may be in place, with limits on flash photography in certain areas to protect delicate artifacts. It's a good idea to check these rules beforehand. Comfortable walking shoes are essential, as the museum's layout includes traversing multiple floors and exhibits.

Enhancing Your Experience

Pairing your visit with a stop at a nearby café or restaurant is a delightful way to think about what you've seen. Many eateries in the area serve traditional Egyptian dishes, offering a chance to enjoy local flavors after your cultural exploration.

WALKING IN THE FOOTSTEPS OF PHARAOHS: INSIDER TIPS FOR ANCIENT SITES

Planning beforehand is crucial while visiting these classic sites. Start with the famous Giza Plateau, home of the Great Pyramid, an ancient marvel that demonstrates the creators' inventiveness. The nearby Sphinx, with its mysterious face, makes one think about the secrets of its beginnings. By getting there early, you may take in these landmarks in a more relaxed setting and absorb their spirit away from the masses.

The Solar Boat Museum nearby provides insight into the funeral customs of ancient kings and queens. Once interred close to the Great Pyramid, the well-preserved vessel serves as evidence of the significance of the afterlife in Egyptian thought. Taking the time to examine its fine craftsmanship can provide details about the pharaohs' spiritual outlook.

A must-see for anybody interested in ancient relics is the Egyptian Museum on Tahrir Square. The riches of

Tutankhamun are part of an unparalleled collection housed in the museum. The displays provide a realistic depiction of life thousands of years ago, from intricate jewelry to enormous statues. To appreciate the depth of the exhibits, set aside a few hours to leisurely peruse the galleries.

A stroll through the medieval streets of Islamic Cairo is a must-do when visiting Cairo's historical landmarks. Even though the neighborhood is mostly linked to later periods, its architecture and layout show an ongoing urban design legacy that extends back thousands of years. The Khan el-Khalili market offers a chance to experience the lively spirit of local culture and appreciate traditional workmanship thanks to its bustling environment and small pathways.

Be mindful of a few useful pointers as you traverse these breathtaking places. It is imperative to wear comfortable walking shoes because many of the paths are uneven, especially in the vicinity of Giza and Saqqara. The Egyptian sun may be very strong, especially in the cooler months, so bring drink and sunscreen. A skilled guide may make a big difference in your trip by providing insights and tales that make the attractions come to life in a way that a guidebook can't.

Egypt's past is further revealed by the trip to Saqqara, the ancient Memphis burial site. The majesty of the buildings of Giza was foreshadowed by the Step Pyramid of Djoser, which was created by architect Imhotep. You may observe the development of pyramid construction and recognize the ingenuity of its builders by exploring this webpage. The surrounding tombs offer insights into the everyday routines and religious rituals of the ancient Egyptians, thanks to their striking engravings.

Although Cairo's historic sites are unquestionably fascinating, the city is a live one that is still thriving. An open mind and respect for local traditions can enhance the enjoyment of your trip. Engaging with locals, sampling regional cuisine, and touring lesser-known neighborhoods might enhance your experience.

CHAPTER 3

3. ISLAMIC CAIRO: A JOURNEY THROUGH FAITH AND ARCHITECTURE

THE CITADEL OF SALADIN AND MOHAMMED ALI MOSQUE

A Fortress of History: The Citadel of Saladin

Built in the 12th century by Salah ad-Din (known as Saladin in the West), this fortress served as a strategic defensive base to defend Cairo from the Crusaders. Its massive walls, towers, and gates highlight medieval Islamic architecture and ingenuity. Walking through its vast courtyards, visitors can feel the historical importance of this site, which once stood as a symbol of strength and resilience.

Today, the Citadel stands as a well-preserved reminder of Cairo's dynamic past, housing a collection of museums and buildings that tell stories spanning centuries. Among these are the Police Museum, the Military Museum, and the Carriage Museum, each giving insights into Egypt's diverse heritage. While wandering through its grounds, be sure to explore the impressive Bab al-Azab gate, a towering structure that has watched countless historical events.

The Mohammed Ali Mosque: A Jewel of Ottoman Design

Perched within the Citadel's complex, the Mohammed Ali Mosque is a masterpiece of Ottoman-style building. Commissioned by Mohammed Ali Pasha in the early 19th century, the mosque is instantly recognizable for its large dome, rising minarets, and alabaster walls. Its grandeur reflects the vision of Mohammed Ali, who tried to leave a lasting legacy as the founder of modern Egypt.

Inside the mosque, the detailed details captivate the eye from the opulent chandeliers to the ornate carvings adorning the walls. The interior is spacious and intended to inspire a sense of tranquility, making it a significant place of worship and a prime example of Islamic art. Don't miss the striking clock tower given by King Louis Philippe of France, although it remains nonfunctional to this day.

Tips for Visiting These Iconic Landmarks

1. Plan Your Visit Early: Arriving in the morning helps you escape the afternoon crowds and enjoy the cooler hours of the day.

2. Wear Comfortable Shoes: Exploring the sprawling grounds of the Citadel involves a fair amount of walking, so sensible footwear is a must.

3. Dress Respectfully: Since the mosque is a busy place of worship, wearing modest clothing is important. Women may need to bring a scarf to cover their heads.

4. Bring Cash: Entry fees are often paid in cash, and having some Egyptian pounds handy will make the process easier.

5. Photograph Wisely: While photography is allowed, be aware of worshippers and avoid using flash inside the mosque. The Citadel also gives panoramic views of Cairo perfect for capturing unforgettable moments.

6. Combine Visits: Consider pairing your trip to the Citadel with other nearby sites, such as Sultan Hassan

Mosque or the vibrant Khan el-Khalili Bazaar, for a full day of exploration.

Why These Sites Are a Must-Visit

The Citadel of Saladin and the Mohammed Ali Mosque encapsulate Cairo's historical layers, mixing military might with artistic grandeur. From the heights of the Citadel, you can see the sprawling city below—a contrast between ancient buildings and modern urban life. The sense of awe these landmarks evoke is unmatched, and they offer visitors a better understanding of Cairo's historical and cultural evolution.

AL-AZHAR MOSQUE AND UNIVERSITY: A CENTER OF ISLAMIC LEARNING

A Historical Perspective

Founded in 970 CE by the Fatimid Caliphate, Al-Azhar Mosque began as a place of worship but quickly became a hub for academic study. Over time, it evolved into one of the oldest and most prestigious centers for Islamic studies, offering a curriculum that covers religious, philosophical, and scientific fields. Its name, derived from "Al-Zahra" (meaning "The Radiant"), celebrates Fatimah Al-Zahra, the daughter of the Prophet Muhammad.

The mosque's architecture shows the evolution of Islamic art over centuries, with intricate details in its minarets, arches, and courtyards. Visitors are often captivated by the craftsmanship, which serves as a living testament to Cairo's place as a center of culture and learning during the Islamic Golden Age.

The Role of Al-Azhar Today

Al-Azhar University, officially formed in 1961, works as an extension of the mosque's legacy, blending traditional Islamic teachings with modern disciplines. It gives programs in fields such as medicine, engineering, and business alongside religious studies, providing a comprehensive educational environment. Scholars and clerics trained here often go on to take prominent roles in global Islamic discourse, underscoring its importance on the world stage.

Visiting Al-Azhar

A visit to Al-Azhar Mosque offers more than a glimpse into history; it's a chance to experience a place that continues to inspire reverence and scholarship. The mosque is open to visitors of all faiths, allowing them to admire its significance and architectural beauty.

Tips for Your Visit

1. Dress Appropriately: Modest clothing is needed to enter the mosque. Women are advised to bring a scarf to cover their hair, and both men and women should wear garments that cover their shoulders and feet.

2. Timing Your Visit: The mosque is open daily, but coming during prayer times allows for a more serene experience. Fridays are particularly special, as they draw larger gatherings for the weekly congregational prayers.

3. Photography: While capturing the beauty of the mosque is urged, ensure you are respectful of worshippers and avoid using flash inside.

4. Local Guides: Hiring a guide can provide a deeper understanding of the mosque's past and its role in Islamic culture.

Costs and Accessibility

Entry to Al-Azhar Mosque is usually free, though donations are appreciated to support its maintenance. If you're hiring a guide, fees usually range between $10 and

$30, based on the duration and level of detail provided. The surrounding area, known as Islamic Cairo, is available by public transportation, including the metro and taxis, making it an easy addition to your Cairo itinerary.

SULTAN HASSAN AND AL-RIFA'I MOSQUES: ARCHITECTURAL WONDERS

The Sultan Hassan Mosque, built in the 14th century, is often regarded as one of the most ambitious building projects of its time. Its towering walls, intricately carved stonework, and immense size make it an iconic building in the city's skyline. Commissioned during the reign of Sultan Hassan, the mosque acted as both a place of worship and a madrasa (Islamic school).

Its design includes four iwans, each devoted to one of the major schools of Sunni Islam, representing the inclusive approach of its era. The inner garden is adorned with fine details, while the monumental dome and towering minaret remain testaments to the craftsmanship of the time.

Across the way lies the Al-Rifa'i Mosque, a masterpiece finished in the early 20th century. Though newer than its neighbor, it complements the Sultan Hassan Mosque with its unique elegance.

The mosque was built to house royal tombs and serves as the resting place for several members of Egypt's royal family, including King Farouk, as well as Iran's Shah Mohammad Reza Pahlavi. The intricate marble work, gilded ceilings, and grand arches display the merging of traditional Islamic architecture with modern techniques, making it a fascinating counterpart to the Sultan Hassan Mosque.

Practical Information for Visitors

Visiting these mosques is both cheap and enriching. Entry fees are usually reasonable, costing around 100 EGP (Egyptian pounds) for foreign tourists, though prices may vary. Tickets often give access to both sites, allowing you to fully explore the area. Local visitors and students may benefit from discounted rates, so it's worth carrying a legal ID or student card.

Both mosques are open to visitors throughout the week, usually from morning until late afternoon. To ensure a pleasant visit, consider coming early in the day to avoid crowds and enjoy the serene atmosphere. Modest attire is important, as these are busy places of worship. Women may be required to cover their hair, and shawls or scarves are often given at the entrance.

Photography is allowed in most areas, but flash and tripods are generally restricted. Respect the quiet ambiance, especially during prayer times, when certain areas may be closed to tourists. Guides are available for hire on-site and can provide a better understanding of the historical and cultural context of these stunning landmarks.

THE MAZE OF KHAN EL-KHALILI BAZAAR: HISTORY MEETS SHOPPING

The origins of the market date back to the 14th century, when it was created during the reign of Sultan Barquq. Initially, the area served as a hub for traders from across the region, trading goods ranging from spices and textiles to valuable metals. Over time, it grew into a thriving marketplace, its labyrinth of narrow alleys filled with the scent of exotic spices and the shimmering colors of handmade crafts. Today, this legacy remains intact, drawing locals and tourists alike into its historic embrace.

Shopping here is an adventure. Visitors can find an array of items, from handmade jewelry and intricately designed lamps to aromatic teas and richly embroidered fabrics.

The artisans who create these goods are often descendants of families who have been plying their skills for generations, adding an authentic and personal touch to every piece. Whether you're seeking a unique keepsake or a meaningful gift, the market offers endless chances to discover something special.

Prices in the market vary greatly, showing the diversity of goods and the importance of bargaining. Many sellers expect some bargaining, and it's considered part of the cultural experience. A good rule of thumb is to start with half the stated price and work your way up. Friendly but firm negotiation often leads to a fair deal for both sides. Visitors who approach the process with respect and humor often leave with not only a great deal but also a memorable story to share.

While visiting the market, it's helpful to come prepared with a few practical tips. First, comfortable footwear is important, as the cobblestone streets and uneven surfaces can make for a long day of walking. Carrying small denominations of cash is also suggested, as many vendors prefer it over credit cards. Staying hydrated and taking occasional breaks at one of the nearby coffeehouses will keep your energy levels high as you cross the lively stalls.

The market's surroundings offer plenty of fascinating sites. The nearby Al-Hussein Mosque is an iconic landmark, steeped in both religious and architectural importance. Its serene atmosphere provides a stark contrast to the lively energy of the market, giving a moment of reflection amidst the excitement. Just a short walk away, visitors can also discover the historic Muizz Street, home to beautifully preserved Islamic architecture.

The market's lively atmosphere comes alive, particularly in the evenings when the glow of lanterns illuminates the stalls and the sounds of live music fill the air. The mix of sights, sounds, and scents forms an ambiance that lingers long after the visit ends. Whether it's the call of a vendor selling handmade goods or the aroma of freshly brewed mint tea wafting from a corner café, the experience leaves a lasting impression.

In many ways, this iconic marketplace is more than just a shopping destination it's a live museum that tells the story of Cairo through its sights and sounds. From its rich past to its dynamic present, it serves as a microcosm of the city itself, reflecting both its timeless traditions and its evolving character. For travelers wanting a connection to

Cairo's cultural roots, exploring this lively bazaar is an essential part of the journey.

CHAPTER 4

4. COPTIC CAIRO: CHRISTIANITY'S FOOTPRINT IN EGYPT

THE HANGING CHURCH: A TESTAMENT TO FAITH

The Hanging Church, located in the heart of Cairo's Coptic district, stands as one of the most revered and historically rich places in Egypt. Officially known as the Saint Virgin Mary's Coptic Orthodox Church, it gets its nickname from its unique architectural feature: the nave is suspended over a passageway that once formed part of a Roman fortress. This iconic structure, going back to the 3rd century, continues to be a symbol of faith and perseverance, drawing visitors with its remarkable history and spiritual significance.

A Historical Treasure

The church's origins trace back to when Christianity was emerging as a dominant religion in Egypt. Built over the ruins of the Babylon Fortress, its location represents resilience in the face of adversity. Over the ages, the site has undergone numerous restorations, preserving its legacy as one of Cairo's oldest Christian churches. Its wooden roof, shaped like Noah's Ark, and intricate icons depicting biblical scenes reflect the ingenuity and devotion of the craftsmen who made them.

Walking through its gates, you'll find yourself transported into a world where faith and artistry mix seamlessly. The church features over 100 icons, each a gem of Coptic art. These intricate depictions, made between the 8th and 18th centuries, tell stories that resonate strongly with visitors, regardless of their religious background.

Spiritual and Cultural Significance

The site holds deep spiritual meaning for the Coptic Christian community. It has long been a place of worship, providing comfort and consistency in a world that is always changing. It was also the residence of the Coptic Orthodox Pope for nearly a thousand years, further cementing its importance in Egyptian Christian history.

Visitors often note the calm ambiance of the church, a sharp contrast to the bustling streets of Cairo. Whether observing a quiet moment of meditation or attending a traditional service, the atmosphere invites a sense of peace and connection.

Tips for Your Visit

To make the most of your time, try arriving early in the morning when the church is less crowded. Modest clothing is suggested as a sign of respect, and photography is usually allowed, but it's always best to confirm any restrictions upon arrival. Engaging a knowledgeable guide can provide deeper insights into the church's past and its cultural context.

The Hanging Church is part of a larger area known as Old Cairo, which houses other important landmarks, including the Ben Ezra Synagogue and the Church of St. Sergius and Bacchus. Planning a visit to these neighboring sites can provide a more comprehensive understanding of Cairo's rich religious past.

Practical Information

The church is open daily, with free entry for visitors, though donations are accepted. Its location is easily accessible by public transportation or taxi, and it's a short walk from the Mar Girgis Metro stop. It should take visitors at least an hour to thoroughly examine the site.

If you're considering buying souvenirs, nearby shops offer a variety of Coptic crosses, religious icons, and other handcrafted items. These make meaningful keepsakes and help local artisans.

Why It's Worth a Visit

The Hanging Church is not merely a historical monument; it's a live testament to the enduring spirit of faith. It serves as a reminder of Egypt's diverse cultural heritage and offers a space where history and spirituality meet. Whether you're exploring its architectural marvels, admiring its ancient artwork, or simply soaking in the peaceful atmosphere, the experience is sure to leave a lasting impression.

THE COPTIC MUSEUM: ARTIFACTS OF A RICH HISTORY

Highlights from the Collection

The museum houses a wide variety of antiquities, including linens, manuscripts, icons, and stone carvings. Among its most renowned treasures are illuminated Bible manuscripts, which have been preserved in extraordinary detail. These manuscripts not only demonstrate the competence of early Coptic scribes but also shed light on the community's spiritual and artistic life.

Another feature is a collection of finely carved wooden panels, many of which were originally part of historic churches. Their designs reflect Coptic art's unique blend of Pharaonic, Greek, Roman, and Byzantine influences. The museum's textile collection, which includes beautiful tapestries and clothing, demonstrates the expertise of early Coptic weavers as well as the significance of textile manufacturing in the community's economic and social life.

The icons on display are another gem, each conveying a story with vivid imagery and symbolic detail. These icons, which are frequently utilized in liturgical contexts, offer a spiritual connection to the past while also reflecting the devotion of the artists who made them.

Practical Tips for Visitors:

1. Visiting Hours: The museum is normally open every day, however, hours may change based on holidays or special events. Arriving early in the day guarantees a quieter atmosphere, allowing you to explore at your leisure.

2. Location and accessibility: The museum is located in Old Cairo and is easily accessible by taxi or public transport. Combining a museum visit with local attractions such as the Hanging Church or the Ben Ezra Synagogue can help you plan a more complete itinerary.

3. Photographic Rules: While photography is normally permitted, it is always advisable to check restrictions at the

gate. Flash photography may be forbidden to protect sensitive artifacts.

Travel Tips for a Smooth Visit

1. Dress comfortably. Dress appropriately for Cairo's climate, particularly during the warmer months. Comfortable shoes are required for exploring the museum and the neighboring historic quarter.

2. Plan Your Visit: Set aside at least two hours to thoroughly appreciate the museum's collection. Combine your visit with a stop at a neighboring café or restaurant to sample local cuisine and refuel.

3. Respect the Space: The museum is more than just a cultural institution; it also has significant historical and religious significance. Approach your tour with respect for the items and the people who made them.

Inspiring a deeper connection.

The museum demonstrates Egypt's Coptic community's tenacity and inventiveness. Each sculpture conveys a tale about survival, adaptation, and the unwavering force of faith. By visiting, visitors not only obtain a better knowledge of this unique cultural heritage but also help to preserve it for future generations.

BEN EZRA SYNAGOGUE: A RARE RELIGIOUS BLEND

The synagogue, which dates from the ninth century, was once a Coptic Christian church before being sold to the Jewish community to pay taxes. Over time, it became one of Egypt's most revered Jewish heritage monuments. Its location near Fustat, known as the cradle of Cairo's ancient towns, adds to its historical significance. The synagogue is famed for the discovery of the Cairo Geniza, a collection of ancient texts that provide unmatched insight into medieval Jewish life in the Mediterranean region.

Stepping inside, guests are met with exquisite architectural components that combine Islamic, Jewish, and Coptic influences. High oak ceilings, finely carved panels, and geometric designs depict a rich tapestry of cultural exchanges throughout centuries. The sacred ark, positioned against the eastern wall, emanates subtle majesty while protecting sacred Torah scrolls. Each feature of the synagogue whispers stories from its vivid past, leaving visitors in amazement.

The synagogue serves as a gateway to comprehending Cairo's profound religious diversity. The neighborhood is a religious crossroads, with notable landmarks like the Hanging Church and Amr ibn al-As Mosque. Together, these landmarks tell a story of harmony and cohabitation that crosses cultures and decades.

Practical information for visitors.

The Egyptian Ministry of Antiquities manages the synagogue as a museum and welcomes visitors. Tickets are fairly priced, making them affordable for vacationers. This historical jewel is accessible for a nominal price, usually between 100 and 120 EGP. Some photography limitations may apply within the building, so it's best to check on-site policies ahead of time.

Tips for a Smooth Visit.

1. Timing: Mornings are best for visiting because the place is less crowded, allowing for a more personal encounter.

2. Dress Code: Respect the area's religious and cultural significance by wearing modest apparel.

3. Guided Tours: Hiring a skilled guide can enhance your visit by providing a better understanding of the site's history and context.

4. Accessibility: While the synagogue is typically well-maintained, several locations may provide difficulties for persons with mobility impairments, therefore planning is encouraged.

THE MONASTERY OF ST. SIMON THE TANNER: HIDDEN IN THE HILLS

The Cave Church, also called the Monastery of St. Simon the Tanner, is a distinctive site tucked away in the Mokattam Hills of Cairo. This extraordinary place is both a spiritual retreat and a testimony to human resilience, with a story that draws people from all over the world. Beyond its theological significance, the monastery is an architectural marvel, sculpted into cliffs and covered with elaborate carvings and murals depicting old tales.

The trek to this location provides a unique perspective on Cairo's rich cultural and religious fabric. The monastery is located near Garbage City, home to the Zabbaleen community, which is well-known for its recycling activities. While the path to the monastery may appear odd at first, it highlights a side of Cairo that is rarely seen, giving visitors a true feel of the city's tenacity and resourcefulness.

When you arrive, you will be astounded by the monastery's massive size. The main auditorium, which can accommodate thousands, is an open-air amphitheater built right into the hillside. The walls are decorated with sculptures and carvings of biblical themes and religious characters, each carefully constructed to express the community's deep devotion and artistry. The monastery's acoustics are another marvel attending a service or event here is a truly touching experience.

Tips for visiting

1. Getting There: Getting to the monastery entails traveling through the Mokattam Hills, which is best accomplished by taking a local taxi or private automobile. As the journey is in a less popular location, make sure your driver is familiar with it.

2. Plan Your Visit: Mornings are the best time to visit because they offer lower temps and a more peaceful ambiance. The monastery is especially stunning around morning when natural light highlights its delicate carvings.

3. Dress Code: As a place of religion, modest attire is advised. Women should carry a scarf to protect their heads, and both men and women should dress appropriately for shoulder and knee coverage.

4. Photography: Taking photos is normally permitted, but always seek permission, particularly during services. Avoid being obtrusive because this is a sacred location for many.

Costs and Entry Fees

The monastery is free to visit, although donations are accepted and benefit the site and the surrounding community. If you decide to hire a guide for a more in-depth tour, the rates will vary but are usually inexpensive.

Local insights

The surrounding area, known as Garbage City, provides an opportunity to learn about the Zabbaleen community's creative garbage management strategies. While investigating, be mindful of the locals' daily lives. Consider supporting local craftsmen by purchasing handcrafted items, which is a meaningful way to give back to the community while also bringing home a unique keepsake.

Why should you visit?

This is more than a religious site; it embodies Cairo's rich history, cultural diversity, and steadfast spirit. Whether you're drawn to the creative carvings, the spiritual atmosphere, or the opportunity to see a different side of the city, the monastery is a visit that will leave an impact.

CHAPTER 5

5. MODERN CAIRO: A CITY OF CONTRASTS

THE NEW ADMINISTRATIVE CAPITAL: CAIRO'S VISION FOR THE FUTURE

The New Administrative Capital is a visionary concept that reimagines Cairo's future by blending innovation, history, and ambition into a single grand project. This growing city, located around 28 miles east of Cairo's bustling metropolis, has the potential to revolutionize Egypt's political, economic, and cultural landscape. It promises to ease the effects of urban overcrowding while demonstrating the capabilities of modern urban design.

At its core, the initiative seeks to combine cutting-edge technology and sustainability. The city boasts vast green spaces, cutting-edge infrastructure, and a commitment to sustainable energy.

The establishment of a consolidated government district, which includes the Presidential Palace, parliament, and supreme court, represents a strategic endeavor to streamline governance and administrative responsibilities.

The center of the New Administrative Capital reflects a future in which progress and tradition coexist together. The central business center is home to Africa's tallest building, the Iconic Tower, which represents Egypt's global ambitions. Meanwhile, educational institutions, superior healthcare facilities, and a variety of leisure alternatives all help to create a balanced metropolitan environment.

This attempt relies heavily on cultural expression. The plans for the Opera House and art galleries show Egypt's desire to preserve its creative past while also encouraging contemporary inventiveness. The huge cultural area pledges to honor the country's rich history while embracing the vibrancy of modern life.

The city boasts one-of-a-kind buildings such as the massive mosque and church, which serve as architectural wonders and symbols of interfaith harmony. With meticulously planned communities, large boulevards, and innovative public transportation systems, it provides a glimpse of what future cities could look like efficient, beautiful, and profoundly connected.

This innovative project is more than simply infrastructure; it signifies a shift in Egypt's vision for growth and prosperity. It embodies the commitment to address long-standing issues, such as congestion and pollution, while also creating a place for the country to thrive in a globalized world.

ZAMALEK: UPSCALE DINING, ART GALLERIES, AND NIGHTLIFE

Upscale Dining

Zamalek has gained a reputation for its culinary excellence, offering a variety of cuisines to please any palate. From elegant restaurants to charming cafés, the area offers a refined eating experience. International flavors sit alongside traditional Egyptian dishes, allowing tourists to savor both the familiar and the exotic. Each venue takes pride in its ambiance, often reflecting the rich cultural history of Cairo while incorporating modern design elements. For travelers, dining in this neighborhood feels like stepping into a crossroads where global and local tastes meet.

Art and Creativity

Art plays a central part in Zamalek's identity. The neighborhood is home to several galleries showcasing contemporary Egyptian talent as well as foreign works. Each space tells a story, giving insights into the region's evolving art scene. A stroll through these galleries is not just about viewing pieces on a wall but interacting with the creative energy that defines Cairo's cultural heartbeat. The area also hosts workshops and events, making it an ideal location for those wanting to connect with the artistic community.

Nightlife and Entertainment

When the sun sets, Zamalek shows yet another side of its personality. The nightlife here runs from laid-back lounges to energetic live music venues, catering to a variety of tastes. Local musicians often share the stage with foreign acts, creating an eclectic and lively atmosphere. Bars and clubs are thoughtfully designed to balance sophistication with fun, ensuring memorable nights for all who visit. For those who prefer a quieter night, many establishments offer cozy areas to relax while enjoying Cairo's skyline.

A Neighborhood Full of Surprises

The streets of Zamalek are lined with unique boutiques, bookshops, and old stores, making it a treasure trove for anyone who loves exploring. These shops often house things you won't find anywhere else, from handcrafted jewelry to rare books. The area's architecture is equally captivating, showing a mix of colonial influences and modern innovation. Walking around Zamalek, you'll notice how effortlessly it balances its rich past with a contemporary edge.

DOWNTOWN CAIRO: HISTORIC STREETS AND MODERN CHARM

Downtown Cairo has a distinct niche in the heart of Egypt's city, with streets that resound with history while embracing modern life. This neighborhood presents a remarkable story of transition and provides a unique viewpoint on Cairo's history over time. From renowned architectural marvels to the bustle of modern city life, this district is a rich tapestry of cultures and eras that will captivate anybody looking to comprehend the city's essence.

The buildings immediately capture your attention. Many of them come from the late nineteenth and early twentieth century and have a mix of European and Egyptian design features. These monuments bear the imprint of French planners who once imagined Cairo as a "Paris on the Nile." The design reflects a time when the city sought to combine local traditions with global ideas. Wide boulevards, elegant balconies, and intricate facades provide unlimited chances for exploration, with each building telling a unique tale.

Tahrir Square, a symbol of revolution and perseverance, is central to this neighborhood. While its name is closely associated with significant national events, it is also a thriving hub surrounded by institutions and landmarks. One of the most noteworthy is the Egyptian Museum, which houses an incredible collection of ancient artifacts. This treasure trove is a must-see for anyone looking to connect with Egypt's rich historical roots, and it's all within walking distance of the district's bustling streets.

The district's beauty extends beyond its historical significance. It thrives with a spirit that combines tradition and innovation. Cafés and bookstores flow onto sidewalks, creating a welcoming environment for both inhabitants and visitors. The region is well-known for its cultural scene, which includes art galleries and theaters that showcase modern voices while also celebrating the city's creative heritage. These locations reveal how the past and present continue to impact one another in profound ways.

A short walk may take you to streets like Talaat Harb or Qasr El-Nil, where you may experience the city's daily pulse. These streets are lined with businesses ranging from old boutiques to modern brands, catering to a wide range of tastes while preserving the authenticity of their surroundings. Not only do the businesses convey stories, but so do the people vendors screaming out their products, pedestrians finding their way, and street performers lending a touch of artistry to the scene.

The transition from day to night is dramatic. The district's lights provide a unique perspective, illuminating its landmarks in a way that highlights their beauty. Rooftop venues and vibrant restaurants are ideal places to end the day, with views of the expansive city and the Nile in the background. Here, you can sense Cairo's heartbeat, a city that never sleeps but constantly adapts and thrives.

This section of the city captures its essence, fusing layers of history with the vitality of today. Each street has its personality, and every bend unveils something new.

CAIRO TOWER: THE BEST VIEWS OF THE CITY

The History Behind the Tower

Built-in the late 1950s, the edifice displays a new vision while still honoring Egypt's rich legacy. The design is inspired by the lotus flower, an old Egyptian symbol, and provides an exquisite touch to the city's skyline. The project, built amid a period of political transition, commemorates a glorious era in Egypt's post-independence history.

What to expect on the observation deck

As you ascend to the observation platform, breathtaking views emerge in all directions. On clear days, the vista reaches far and broad, highlighting the vivid contrasts between Cairo's districts. You'll see the meandering Nile River cutting through the city, ancient sites like the Pyramids of Giza on the horizon, and the architectural wonders of downtown Cairo up close. Visiting around sunset adds a lovely glow to the experience, as the city transforms into shades of gold and scarlet.

Pricing and Visitor Tips

Tickets to the tower are moderately priced, giving it an affordable experience for the majority of guests. While costs may vary significantly, the general admission fee for international tourists is usually around 200 EGP, with discounts available for Egyptian nationals. Children also benefit from discounted pricing, making it a family-friendly experience.

Here are some suggestions to make the most of your visit:

1. Arrive early or late in the day: The tower may be crowded, especially during peak tourist seasons, so visit early in the morning or shortly before sunset for shorter lines and a more relaxing ambiance.

2. Bring a camera: Whether you're a beginner or an experienced photographer, the views from the summit are ideal for capturing amazing moments.

3. Check the weather: Clear skies provide the finest opportunity to enjoy uninterrupted vistas. Hazy days may hide some of the city's details.

4. Plan a meal: Consider dining at the revolving restaurant near the top of the tower. While the cuisine is pricey, the experience of dining with the ever-changing vistas of Cairo is worth it.

Practical information

The Cairo Tower is strategically positioned in the Zamalek district, making it easily accessible from most areas of the city. Public transportation, taxis, and ride-sharing services provide easy access. The tower is open every day, often from dawn until late evening, giving visitors flexibility.

Why It is Worth Visiting

The Cairo Tower is more than just a viewing point for the city; it is a destination that connects the city's past, present, and future. The architecture honors Egypt's creative past, while the views highlight the lively pulse of modern Cairo.

Visiting this monument is more than just sightseeing; it is also about comprehending the city's character.

EXPERIENCES IN THE EGYPTIAN OPERA HOUSE

What to Expect

The Opera House is home to a variety of events, including ballet, orchestral concerts, traditional Arabic music, theater, and contemporary shows. The grand hall, with its impeccable acoustics and elegant design, provides an atmosphere that elevates every show. Visitors are often captivated by the professionalism and artistry displayed on stage, which reflects the devotion of Egypt's artistic community.

Ticket Prices

Ticket prices at the Opera House are surprisingly accessible, making it a must-visit even for budget-conscious tourists. Prices usually range from $5 to $30, depending on the event and seating choice. Premium performances, such as international ballet or symphony orchestras, may cost more but stay affordable compared to similar venues worldwide. Tickets can be bought online or at the box office, though it's wise to book in advance for popular events.

Tips for an Enjoyable Visit

1. Plan Ahead: Review the schedule on the official website to find a show that interests you. Events are announced weeks in advance, giving ample time for planning.

2. Dress Code: While the venue does not require a strict dress code, choosing smart casual attire enhances the experience and aligns with the setting's sophisticated ambiance.

3. Arrival Time: Arrive at least 30 minutes before the performance starts. This gives you time to explore the grounds, locate your seat, and soak in the venue's architecture.

4. Cultural Etiquette: Appreciate the efforts of the artists by refraining from using mobile devices during the show.

Applause at appropriate times is a meaningful way to show respect.

5. Refreshments: Light snacks and beverages are available at the Opera House café, but it's best to enjoy a good meal before or after the performance.

Insider Insights

The Opera House is not just about performances; it's a culture hub. The grounds include art galleries and workshops, where you can glimpse Egypt's creative heart beyond the stage. These venues frequently hold community gatherings and exhibitions that highlight regional creativity and art. Engaging with these activities can add depth to your visit and provide a broader view of Egyptian culture.

CHAPTER 6

6. BEYOND THE CLASSICS: HIDDEN GEMS AND DAY TRIPS

AL-AZHAR PARK: A GREEN OASIS AMID THE URBAN BUZZ

History and Transformation

The park's creation is a testament to vision and determination. Built-in the early 2000s as part of a large-scale urban restoration project, its development was led by the Aga Khan Trust for Culture. The initiative tried to restore life to an area that had long been overlooked, turning it into a source of pride for the community. The result is a 74-acre park filled with lush lawns, fountains, and carefully planned landscapes, all harmonizing with the nearby heritage.

What to Expect

Visitors to this urban retreat are greeted by meticulously kept gardens showcasing plants native to the region, interspersed with shaded walkways and water features.

The layout is carefully designed, making it an inviting spot for strolls or simply relaxing on the grass with family and friends. The park's elevated position gives sweeping views of Cairo, including landmarks like the Citadel and the historic mosques of Islamic Cairo.

In the evening, the setting sun throws a golden glow over the city, creating a tranquil atmosphere that feels worlds away from the bustling streets below. The design of the park includes elements inspired by traditional Islamic gardens, with symmetrical layouts and flowing water adding to its peaceful charm.

Activities and Attractions

Al-Azhar Park is more than just a green space; it serves as a hub for cultural and recreational events. Throughout the year, it hosts music performances, art exhibitions, and other community events that draw people from all walks of life. Families often meet here for picnics, while couples enjoy romantic walks along the beautifully lit pathways after dusk.

One of the park's standout features is its proximity to Cairo's historic area. From here, it's easy to discover nearby attractions like Khan El Khalili, Al-Hussein Mosque, and the many architectural gems of Old Cairo.

Dining Options

The park offers a selection of dining choices that cater to various tastes. The restaurants here provide both traditional Egyptian dishes and foreign cuisine, often accompanied by views of the park's greenery and the Cairo skyline. Whether you're craving a hearty local meal or a lighter choice, the park's dining establishments ensure a satisfying experience.

Entrance Fees and Practical Tips

Access to Al-Azhar Park is budget-friendly, with entrance fees usually costing around 30 Egyptian Pounds for locals and 50 Egyptian Pounds for foreigners. These prices may change slightly, so it's always a good idea to check for updated information before your visit.

To make the most of your time, consider arriving early in the day to escape crowds, especially during weekends and public holidays. Comfortable footwear is suggested, as the park's size requires some walking to fully explore its beauty. Bring a reusable water bottle to stay hydrated, especially during the warmer months.

GARBAGE CITY AND THE CAVE CHURCHES: A DIFFERENT PERSPECTIVE

A Glimpse into Life in Garbage City

This place has become synonymous with recycling and ingenuity. The Zabbaleen community, mainly responsible for the neighborhood's activities, has turned the collection and processing of waste into a sustainable livelihood. For decades, this group has sorted through Cairo's trash, recycling up to 80% of what they collect a figure that surpasses many modern waste management systems worldwide.

While piles of materials line the roads, there's a surprising amount of efficiency in the way everything is handled.

Children and adults alike work together, sorting, cleaning, and repurposing things. Visitors who explore the area with an open mind will find themselves inspired by the community's creativity and drive.

The Cave Churches of Mokattam Mountain

At the heart of Garbage City sits one of Cairo's most remarkable spiritual landmarks: the Cave Churches of Mokattam. The Monastery of Saint Simon the Tanner, carved into the side of the rock, stands as a testament to faith and perseverance. This massive amphitheater-style church can handle thousands of worshippers, making it one of the largest Christian worship places in the Middle East.

The intricate carvings on the church's walls show biblical stories, adding a layer of artistry to the already awe-inspiring site. Visitors often find the serene mood here a stark contrast to the vibrant energy of the city below. Attending a service or simply sitting in a quiet space can be a truly moving experience.

Planning Your Visit

To make the most of a trip to this unique place, it's best to plan. Many tourists choose to hire a local guide familiar with the neighborhood to help navigate its maze-like streets and provide insights into its history and daily life. Guided trips often include transportation, which can be especially useful for those unfamiliar with Cairo's traffic.

Entry to the Cave Churches is usually free, but donations are welcome to help maintain the site. If you're considering a guided tour, prices can vary based on the provider, with rates averaging between $20 and $50 per person. Be sure to confirm whether transportation and extra stops are included in the package.

Tips for a Meaningful Experience

1. Dress Modestly: Respect the cultural norms by wearing modest clothes, especially when visiting the church or interacting with the local community.

2. Bring Small Bills: If you plan to make donations or buy things from local vendors, having smaller denominations of Egyptian pounds on hand is helpful.

3. Be Respectful: Remember, this is not just a tourist attraction but a real neighborhood where people live and work. Engage with the community carefully.

4. Use a Trusted Guide: Opt for a reputable guide to ensure safety and gain a deeper knowledge of the area.

WADI DEGLA PROTECTORATE: HIKING AND NATURE NEAR THE CITY

Overview of the Protectorate

Located southeast of Cairo, Wadi Degla spans an impressive 30 kilometers, showing a desert valley formed millions of years ago. The area is home to limestone cliffs, caves, and a variety of fossils, some going back to the Eocene period. This protected zone supports various flora and fauna, including desert foxes, hares, reptiles, and migratory birds. The combination of natural beauty and ecological significance makes it a rewarding location for those wanting a connection with the outdoors.

Activities to Enjoy

Hiking is the main draw for guests, with trails that vary in difficulty to suit all fitness levels. Whether you're looking for a stroll or a challenging trek, the serene environment of the protectorate offers a refreshing contrast to Cairo's fast pace. The marked paths ensure safety while guiding you through the striking desert scenery.

Cycling is another popular sport, with the wide paths making it easy for bikers to navigate. Renting a bike or bringing your own allows you to explore the area at your own pace, taking in the dramatic views and quiet surroundings.

Wadi Degla is a great spot. The lack of light pollution offers clear skies, ideal for observing constellations. Many visitors also enjoy picnics or simply relaxing under the open sky, enjoying the stillness of the desert.

Entry and Practical Information

The entry fee for Wadi Degla is modest, making it an affordable choice for a day out. As of the most current updates, the cost for Egyptians and residents is around 10 EGP per person, with slightly higher fees for foreigners. Parking is available at an additional charge, and it's advisable to take cash for the entrance fees, as electronic payment may not be accepted.

The protectorate is open year-round, but the best times to come are during the cooler months, from October to April when temperatures are more pleasant. Early mornings and late afternoons are best for avoiding the midday heat.

Tips for a Great Visit

1. Plan: Make sure to check the weather forecast and choose a suitable time to visit. Bring plenty of water, sunscreen, and a hat to protect yourself from the sun.

2. Dress Comfortably: Lightweight clothing and sturdy shoes are important for hiking and exploring the rocky terrain.

3. Stay Safe: Stick to the marked trails and avoid wandering into uncharted places. Bringing a basic first-aid kit is always a good idea for outdoor activities.

4. Pack Snacks: There are no food vendors inside the reserve, so carrying your own snacks or a picnic is suggested. Be mindful of leaving no trash behind to protect the area's natural beauty.

5. Use a Guide: If you're unfamiliar with the area or prefer a more informative experience, local guides are available.

They can enhance your visit by describing the geology and pointing out wildlife you might otherwise miss.

6. Capture the Moment: Bring a camera or smartphone to record the stunning vistas and unique rock formations. The landscape offers a dramatic backdrop for photography enthusiasts.

Accessibility and Getting There

Located about 20 minutes from Cairo's Maadi district, Wadi Degla is easily reachable by car. Hiring a private taxi or using a ride-sharing service is the most convenient choice, though adventurous visitors may decide for public transportation and walk the final stretch.

FAYOUM OASIS AND WADI EL-HITAN: A UNESCO FOSSIL SITE

Fayoum Oasis: A Natural Haven

Fayoum Oasis is an expansive area known for its lush greenery, abundant water sources, and traditional Egyptian charm. The oasis is fed by the waters of Lake Qarun, one of Egypt's oldest natural lakes, which has supported life in the area for thousands of years. Visitors often find solace in the area's serene atmosphere, where palm groves, ancient villages, and historic sites come together harmoniously.

Among the highlights of Fayoum is the Valley of the Whales, known locally as Wadi El-Hitan. This UNESCO World Heritage Site is a testament to Egypt's prehistoric era, giving insights into how marine life once thrived in what is now a vast desert.

Wadi El-Hitan: A Fossil Wonderland

Wadi El-Hitan, or the Valley of the Whales, is an extraordinary paleontological site showing well-preserved fossils of ancient marine creatures. These fossils, mainly of early whale species, date back millions of years and serve as crucial evidence of the evolutionary transition from land-based mammals to ocean-dwelling creatures. The site features well-marked trails that allow visitors to discover the fossils while respecting the delicate environment.

The surrounding desert scenery offers a breathtaking backdrop, with undulating dunes and dramatic rock formations adding to the area's allure. Visiting Wadi El-Hitan provides a chance to connect with a fascinating time in Earth's history, making it a must-see for nature enthusiasts and history buffs alike.

Practical Information

How to Get There

Fayoum Oasis and Wadi El-Hitan are accessible via road from Cairo, making it a handy day trip or overnight destination. Hiring a private car or taking a guided tour is suggested for ease of travel, as public transportation options are limited. Most tours include stops at key places within Fayoum, such as Lake Qarun, Tunis Village, and Wadi El-Hitan.

Entry Fees and Operating Hours

Wadi El-Hitan charges an entry fee that funds the site's preservation efforts. Prices change based on nationality and whether visitors opt for a guided tour. It's wise to check for the latest information from reputable travel providers or official tourism websites to avoid surprises. The site is usually open during daylight hours, with the best time to visit is early morning or late afternoon when temperatures are more manageable.

Tips for a Memorable Visit

1. Pack Essentials: The area's remote nature means facilities are restricted, so bringing plenty of water, snacks, sunscreen, and sturdy footwear is important. A wide-brimmed hat and sunglasses can also help protect against the sun.

2. Choose the Right Time: Fayoum and Wadi El-Hitan are best visited in the cooler months, from October to April. The desert heat can be intense during summer, making exploring less comfortable.

3. Respect the Environment: The fossils at Wadi El-Hitan are priceless treasures. Avoid touching or disturbing them and follow designated paths to minimize environmental effects.

4. Combine with Other Attractions: Fayoum offers other highlights worth discovering, such as the historic pyramids at Hawara and the artistic charm of Tunis Village. These can add depth to your trip and provide a well-rounded experience.

CHAPTER 7

7. THE CULINARY DELIGHTS OF CAIRO

CLASSIC EGYPTIAN DISHES YOU MUST TRY

Koshari, a substantial combination of rice, lentils, and macaroni garnished with a zesty tomato sauce, crunchy fried onions, and a splash of seasoned vinegar, is among the most well-known dishes you'll come across.

This dish's robust flavors and textural combination make it a favorite. In search of a filling and reasonably priced supper, locals frequently form lines at little koshari stores. It is a mainstay that exemplifies Egypt's capacity to create remarkable things out of common elements.

Another traditional meal that has a unique place in Egyptian homes is ful medames. This popular morning meal is made with slow-cooked fava beans and seasoned with lemon, olive oil, and a touch of cumin. Full medames, which are served with warm bread, fresh vegetables, or even a cooked egg, embody the spirit of traditional Egyptian cooking: they are simple yet incredibly filling.

Molokhia, a dish that many Egyptians associate with their homeland, is a must-try when exploring Egyptian cuisine. Jute leaves are used to make this green, leafy soup, which is cooked with coriander, garlic, and occasionally chicken or rabbit stock. Generations have savored its distinct flavor and texture. This dish's versatility and diversity are demonstrated by the various ways that different households prepare it.

Ta'ameya is a must-try for a fast bite on the run or a savory snack. Often referred to as Egypt's falafel, it is cooked with fava beans rather than chickpeas, giving it a bright green hue and a lighter texture. The ideal harmony of flavors is achieved when these crispy patties are served with fresh salad and tahini sauce over warm pita bread. Locals love it, particularly in the mornings.

Rich and savory desserts are another thing that Egyptians are famous for. Made from semolina steeped in sweet syrup and frequently topped with coconut or almonds, basbousa is a unique dessert. It is a favorite choice for festivals or as a hearty way to end a meal because of its rich texture and syrupy sweetness. Om Ali, a baked bread pudding with layers of dough, milk, sugar, and nuts, is another popular choice. This dessert demonstrates the inventiveness of Egyptian chefs and is both decadent and filling.

Even while these foods are well-known, Cairo's thriving eating scene offers a vast array of other cuisines to try. You may experience the essence of Egypt's cuisine through historic restaurants, busy marketplaces, and street vendors. Every morsel serves as a link to the past and a reminder of the various forces that have molded this extraordinary city.

BEST STREET FOOD SPOTS IN CAIRO: FROM KOSHARI TO FALAFEL

1. El Tahrir Koshary

Located in downtown Cairo, this bustling eatery is a must-visit for a taste of koshary, Egypt's national dish. A hearty mix of lentils, rice, pasta, and chickpeas topped with tangy tomato sauce and crispy onions, it's both filling and delicious. Prices typically range from 15 to 30 EGP, depending on portion size. The experience of watching the staff skillfully assemble your bowl is as satisfying as the dish itself.

2. Felfela Takeaway

Known for its quick service and freshly made falafel, Felfela has been a favorite for decades. Egyptian falafel, made from fava beans rather than chickpeas, boasts a unique flavor. Pair it with tahini sauce and pickled vegetables for a perfect snack or meal. Sandwiches cost around 10 to 20 EGP, making it an affordable option for a quick bite.

3. Gad Restaurant

While Gad offers sit-down dining, its takeaway window is where the street food magic happens. Try the stuffed pita sandwiches filled with kofta, liver, or falafel. The variety ensures there's something for everyone, and prices start at 15 EGP for a sandwich. The freshness of the ingredients and the bold flavors make it a standout choice.

4. Zooba

A modern twist on traditional Egyptian street food, Zooba is perfect for those who appreciate innovation in their meals. With options like koshary, hawawshi, and falafel served in colorful, eco-friendly packaging, it's both stylish and authentic. Expect to pay slightly more here, with dishes ranging from 25 to 50 EGP, but the quality and presentation make it worth it.

5. Koshary Abou Tarek

A legendary spot in Cairo, Abou Tarek has built a reputation for serving some of the city's finest koshary. It is a favorite among both locals and tourists because of the vibrant atmosphere and hearty quantities. Prices range between 20 and 40 EGP, depending on how hungry you are. Don't forget to drizzle their homemade garlic vinegar and spicy chili sauce over your dish for an extra kick.

6. Akl Zaman

This hidden gem is known for its delicious hawawshi a crispy bread stuffed with spiced minced meat and baked to perfection. Served hot and packed with flavor, it's a treat that's hard to resist. Prices are affordable, starting at around 20 EGP. The vendor's dedication to using fresh ingredients adds a special touch to every bite.

7. Street Vendors in Khan El Khalili

While exploring the vibrant bazaar of Khan El Khalili, you'll encounter numerous vendors offering everything from grilled corn to sweet pastries. Stop by for a fresh baladi bread sandwich filled with spiced liver or a cup of sugar-dusted zalabia (fried dough). Prices vary but are generally pocket-friendly, with snacks costing as little as 5 EGP.

FINE DINING EXPERIENCES WITH A VIEW OF THE NILE

Dining by the Nile: A Blend of Flavors and Atmosphere

Cairo's restaurant scene captures the diversity of the city itself, blending Middle Eastern traditions with foreign influences. Along the riverbanks, establishments cater to a variety of tastes, offering everything from perfectly prepared Egyptian dishes to global cuisines. Each setting offers something unique, whether it's the lively cityscape shimmering in the distance or the gentle sway of feluccas passing under a moonlit sky.

The Allure of Riverside Dining Dining by the Nile isn't just about the food it's an experience that connects the senses. Many places feature terraces or open-air seating, where the soft breeze complements the aroma of freshly prepared dishes. Candlelit tables along the waterfront create a romantic atmosphere, while roomy setups with panoramic windows offer a cozy yet refined environment for groups.

Highlights of the Culinary Scene

Several notable establishments stand out for their exceptional food and commitment to creating memorable dining moments. At these locations, chefs carefully create menus that celebrate local ingredients and culinary traditions while presenting dishes with an artistic touch. Whether it's freshly caught seafood paired with seasonal veggies or aromatic spices elevating a simple dish to a gourmet experience, these meals leave a lasting impression.

Seasonal Dining and Special Events

Seasonal menus and events often improve the draw of riverside dining. Many places hold live music nights, themed dinners, or cultural celebrations that allow guests to savor the essence of Cairo uniquely. From sipping a perfectly brewed cup of tea during sunset to having a multi-course feast under the stars, there's always an occasion to celebrate by the water.

Practical Tips for a Perfect Evening

To fully enjoy the experience, consider reserving a table in advance, especially during weekends or holiday seasons when popular spots fill quickly. Arriving slightly early provides an opportunity to take in the view before the meal starts. Dress codes may range, so it's worth checking with the restaurant beforehand to match the ambiance.

Take time to explore the dessert choices. Many establishments offer sweet creations inspired by Egyptian and Mediterranean customs, providing the perfect ending to an already delightful experience.

MARKETS, CAFES, AND DESSERT SHOPS: SATISFYING YOUR SWEET TOOTH

Exploring Markets for Authentic Sweets

The city's bustling bazaars are not only a haven for spices, textiles, and gifts but also for traditional confections that have stood the test of time. Khan El Khalili, one of Cairo's most famous markets, is an excellent place to start. Vendors offer a range of sweets like baklava, kunafa, and basbousa, each showing layers of flavor crafted with ingredients such as honey, nuts, and semolina.

These treats are often sold by weight, with prices usually ranging from $5 to $10 per kilogram, depending on the quality and variety. To get the freshest selections, try coming in the morning or late afternoon when stock turnover is at its peak.

Cafes Offering a Blend of Tradition and Modernity

Cafes in Cairo are more than just places to grab a quick bite; they're cultural hubs where locals and tourists meet to unwind. Many feature menus brimming with both traditional Egyptian desserts and modern versions. A standout choice is Naguib Mahfouz Café, located in the heart of the historic district. Here, you can enjoy a slice of umm ali a warm, pudding-like dish made with puff pastry, milk, and nuts for around $4 to $6, followed by a rich cup of mint tea. The serene atmosphere makes it a great spot to take a break from sightseeing.

Head to Cake Café in Zamalek. Known for its chic décor and creative offerings, this spot serves everything from macarons to handmade chocolates. Prices are slightly higher, usually $3 to $5 per item, but the quality and presentation make it worth the splurge.

Specialty Dessert Shops Worth Visiting

Cairo is home to countless shops dedicated to making sweets with precision and care. One must-visit location is El Abd, a local institution famous for its wide collection of pastries and candies. From freshly made kahk (shortbread cookies filled with dates or nuts) to creamy rice pudding, every bite is a testament to generations of skill. Prices here are budget-friendly, with most things costing between $2 and $7.

Another gem is Mandarine Koueider, a family-run business renowned for its ice cream and oriental sweets. Their mango sorbet and pistachio baklava are fan favorites. With desserts priced around $2 to $5 per serving, it's an accessible treat for travelers on any income.

Insider Tips for a Sweet Experience

1. Timing Matters: Many dessert shops and cafes experience rush hours, especially after dinner. Visiting earlier in the day often means quicker service and fresher offerings.

2. Sharing servings: Egyptian desserts are known for their richness, and servings can be generous. Sharing with a friend or taking leftovers is a sensible way to try more flavors.

3. Local Recommendations: Don't hesitate to ask locals for their favorite places. They often know the best secret gems that aren't listed in guidebooks.

4. Takeaway Options: Many shops offer beautifully packaged sweets that make excellent gifts or keepsakes. Be sure to check packaging choices if you're planning to bring a taste of Cairo back home.

COOKING CLASSES: LEARN HOW TO BRING EGYPT'S FLAVORS HOME

Locations

Cairo offers a variety of settings for these experiences, ranging from intimate classes held in local homes to professional culinary schools. Some well-known choices include venues in historic districts, where the city's culture adds an extra layer of depth to the activity. Many instructors have deep roots in Egyptian cooking, giving not only recipes but also personal anecdotes and tips about ingredients and preparation methods.

Prices

The cost of a class can vary based on the location, instructor, and length. Private sessions in local homes tend to be more intimate and moderately priced, while professional workshops in larger kitchens might cost a bit more due to the use of advanced tools and larger group settings. On average, prices range from $30 to $100 per person, based on the inclusions, such as the variety of dishes taught and the length of the session. It's wise to confirm what is covered ingredients, meals, and any take-home recipes before booking.

Tips

1. Choose a Class That Fits Your Schedule: Some sessions are meant for a few hours, while others may span an entire day. Shorter classes generally focus on one or two recipes, while longer ones offer a more in-depth experience.

2. Ask About Dietary Preferences: If you have specific preferences or restrictions, such as vegetarian or gluten-free choices, ask the instructor beforehand. Many lessons are adaptable to individual needs.

3. Bring Comfortable Clothing: Since the process can involve active involvement, it's a good idea to dress

comfortably and bring an apron if the class doesn't provide one.

4. Learn About Local Ingredients: Many courses include a visit to local markets, where participants can see, touch, and buy unique spices and produce. These trips are a great way to familiarize yourself with ingredients that are staples in Egyptian kitchens.

5. Take Notes: While instructors often provide written recipes, jotting down your thoughts about methods or variations can make replicating the dishes at home easier.

6. Engage with the Instructor: Don't hesitate to ask questions about the history of the dishes or alternative ways to make them. Many instructors enjoy sharing cultural insights alongside their culinary knowledge.

CHAPTER 8

8. SHOPPING AND SOUVENIRS

TRADITIONAL MARKETS: KHAN EL-KHALILI AND MORE

Khan el-Khalili: A Glimpse into Cairo's Heritage

Khan el-Khalili is more than a marketplace; it is a window into Egypt's historical and cultural soul. Established in the 14th century, the market retains its medieval charm, with winding alleys lined by shops brimming with goods that reflect the nation's diverse traditions. Visitors can find everything from handcrafted jewelry and intricate metalwork to vibrant textiles, perfumes, and spices. It's a space where artisans keep age-old crafts alive while sharing stories of their work with curious shoppers.

Key Details

Location: The market is located in the heart of Islamic Cairo, close to Al-Azhar Mosque and other historical landmarks.

Hours: Typically open daily from 9 AM to late evening. Fridays may have shorter hours due to prayers.

Best Time to Visit: Early mornings or late afternoons tend to be less crowded and more enjoyable for exploring.

Exploring Beyond Khan el-Khalili

While this market is the crown jewel of Cairo's bazaars, several other traditional markets are worth visiting:

1. Souq al-Gomaa (Friday Market)

A bustling flea market held every Friday in the Sayeda Aisha district, this market is an eclectic treasure trove. Shoppers can find antiques, household items, and unique collectibles.

Location: Sayeda Aisha district

Hours: Fridays, sunrise to early afternoon

Tip: Arrive early for the best finds and bring cash, as most vendors don't accept cards.

2. Wekalet El Balah

This market specializes in fabrics and garments, from traditional clothing to modern designs. It's an excellent spot for sourcing affordable and high-quality textiles.

Location: Boulaq neighborhood, near the Nile Corniche

Hours: Open daily, 10 AM to 8 PM

Tip: Don't hesitate to negotiate prices, as bargaining is customary.

3. Ataba Market

Known for its affordability, Ataba Market offers a wide range of goods, including electronics, stationery, and household items.

Location: Central Cairo, near the Opera Square

Hours: Daily, from morning until late evening

Tip: The market can get crowded, so consider visiting during weekdays for a more relaxed experience.

MODERN MALLS: WHERE THE LOCALS SHOP

Key Locations and Highlights

1. Cairo Festival City Mall

Situated in the bustling New Cairo district, this expansive complex is one of the city's most prominent shopping destinations. With over 300 stores, it caters to various preferences, from high-end fashion to affordable everyday items. Popular brands such as Zara, H&M, and Adidas are found here, alongside local Egyptian boutiques offering unique handcrafted goods.

The mall also features an outdoor promenade with fountains, making it a pleasant space to relax. Dining options range from international franchises to traditional Egyptian eateries. Prices in the stores vary widely, ensuring something for every budget. To avoid the crowds, weekday mornings are ideal for a visit.

2. Mall of Egypt

Located along Al Wahat Road in the 6th of October City, this complex stands out for its wide array of entertainment options. Home to the region's only indoor ski slope, it's a magnet for families and those seeking leisure beyond shopping. The mall also boasts a large multiplex cinema and an extensive food court. Shoppers can browse a mix of luxury retailers and mid-tier stores, ensuring diverse offerings. Dining here ranges from casual fast food to upscale restaurants serving global cuisines. Parking is plentiful, but arriving early is advised, especially on weekends.

3. Citystars Heliopolis

Among Cairo's most well-established malls, this shopping center in the Heliopolis district has been a local favorite for years. Spanning several levels, it offers a mix of retail, dining, and entertainment. Stores include popular global brands and niche outlets for souvenirs and specialty items. The top floor features an array of eateries, from budget-friendly options to more refined dining experiences. A highlight is the cinema complex, which often screens the latest international blockbusters. Keep an eye out for seasonal sales, which can offer significant discounts.

Tips for a Seamless Experience

1. Timing Your Visit: Weekends tend to draw larger crowds, so visiting on weekdays can provide a more relaxed experience. Early mornings or late afternoons are often quieter.

2. Transportation: Ride-hailing apps like Uber and Careem are widely available and convenient for reaching most malls. Public transport is an option, but it may be less reliable depending on your location.

3. Currency and Payments: While most outlets accept credit cards, carrying some Egyptian pounds in cash is advisable for smaller shops or kiosks.

4. Dress Comfortably: Cairo's weather can be warm, so wear light clothing and comfortable shoes, especially if you plan to explore larger complexes.

5. Explore Beyond Retail: Many of these locations host events such as art exhibitions, food festivals, and live music performances. Check the mall's website or social media pages for updates.

WHAT TO BUY: FROM PAPYRUS ART TO GOLD JEWELRY

Papyrus Art: A Timeless Memento

Papyrus art makes for a meaningful keepsake that reflects Egypt's ancient heritage. These artworks, crafted on paper made from the papyrus plant, often depict pharaohs, gods, and scenes from Egyptian mythology.

You'll find authentic papyrus art at reputable galleries like the Papyrus Institute or shops in the Khan El Khalili bazaar. Prices typically range from $10 to $100, depending on size and intricacy. Always verify authenticity by ensuring the papyrus fibers are visible when held up to light. Bargaining is common, so don't hesitate to negotiate a fair deal.

Gold Jewelry: A Symbol of Elegance

Egyptian gold jewelry is renowned for its exceptional purity and intricate designs. From delicate pendants to ornate bracelets, these pieces are both a fashion statement and an investment. The Gold Souk in Khan El Khalili and upscale stores in areas like Zamalek are prime spots for finding authentic items. Prices vary widely based on weight and craftsmanship but expect to pay approximately $50 per gram for high-quality gold. Always ask for a purity certificate and check for hallmark stamps to ensure authenticity. Skilled negotiation can help you secure a better price without compromising on quality.

Perfume Oils: The Essence of Tradition

Egyptian perfume oils, known as attar, offer a sensory journey into the country's rich olfactory heritage. These oils, derived from natural ingredients, are long-lasting and free of alcohol, making them ideal for personal use or gifts. Shops like Giza Perfumes Palace and other well-known outlets in the city offer an impressive variety of scents, from floral to musky. Small bottles start at $5, with larger, more refined options costing upwards of $50. Ensure you sample the oils before purchasing, and always confirm they are alcohol-free.

Handcrafted Rugs and Carpets: A Statement Piece

Handmade rugs and carpets showcase Egypt's artistry and attention to detail. Each piece tells a story, with patterns inspired by local culture. The Tentmakers' Bazaar, known as Suq Al Khayamiya, is a great place to find intricately designed textiles. Prices vary depending on size, material, and craftsmanship, typically ranging from $100 to several thousand dollars. If you're buying a larger piece, inquire about shipping options to avoid carrying bulky items during your travels.

Alabaster and Stoneware: Earthy Elegance

Consider alabaster or other handcrafted stoneware. These items, which include vases, bowls, and decorative sculptures, are made from locally sourced materials. Shops near Giza and Luxor often specialize in these crafts. Prices range from $20 to $300, depending on size and complexity. To ensure you're buying genuine alabaster, feel the weight and texture of the item authentic pieces are smooth and cool to the touch.

Cotton Products: Soft and Luxurious

Egyptian cotton is celebrated worldwide for its quality and softness. From bed linens to scarves, these items are practical and luxurious. Stores like Nefertari and others in downtown Cairo offer a variety of cotton goods at competitive prices. Expect to pay around $20 for smaller items like scarves and significantly more for high-thread-count sheets. Always check for a label confirming the product is 100% Egyptian cotton.

Shopping Tips

1. Haggle respectfully: Bargaining is part of the shopping culture in Cairo, especially in bazaars. Begin with an offer that's about half of the initial price and work your way to a mutually acceptable amount.

2. Carry cash: While many shops accept cards, smaller vendors often prefer cash, particularly Egyptian pounds.

3. Shop early: Visiting markets in the morning allows you to explore without the large crowds that gather later in the day.

4. Beware of counterfeits: Stick to reputable vendors to avoid buying fake or low-quality items.

5. Pack wisely: If you're purchasing fragile items like alabaster or papyrus art, request proper wrapping or packaging to protect them during your travels.

TIPS FOR BARGAINING LIKE A LOCAL

Understand the Process

Bargaining is woven into the fabric of Cairo's markets. Sellers often start with a higher price, expecting that buyers will counter with a lower offer. The final price normally lands somewhere in between. This practice isn't about tricking customers but building an interactive exchange. It's important to approach negotiations with a lighthearted attitude and enjoy the process rather than focusing solely on the result.

Research Before You Shop

Before venturing into Cairo's markets, spend some time understanding what items usually cost. Whether you're shopping for handmade jewelry, textiles, or spices, knowing a reasonable price range gives you a good starting point. Speak with locals or your hotel staff for ideas or check nearby fixed-price stores to get a baseline.

Start with a Smile

A warm, friendly approach goes a long way in building goodwill. Greeting the seller in Arabic, even with a simple "Salam Alaikum" (peace be upon you), can set a good tone. Building rapport helps make a more enjoyable experience and might even lead to better prices.

Be Polite, Yet Firm

Keep your demeanor courteous while communicating your preferred price. Avoid appearing too eager, as this can weaken your situation. A calm and confident attitude suggests that you are familiar with the process and unwilling to overpay.

Offer a Counter Price

When the seller offers a price, respond with a number lower than what you're willing to pay. This creates room to meet in the middle, which is often where both sides find common ground. For instance, if the seller starts at 200 Egyptian pounds, you might counter with 100, knowing you're fine settling at 150.

Use Silence to Your Advantage

Silence can be a powerful tool during talks. If a seller isn't budging on the price, take a moment to stop and consider your next move. Sometimes, your silence encourages them to give a better deal to keep the conversation going.

Walk Away When Necessary

One of the most successful bargaining techniques is the willingness to walk away. If the price isn't meeting your goals or you sense the seller won't lower it further, politely thank them and start to leave. Often, this will cause them to call you back with a more reasonable offer.

Pay Attention to the Currency

When agreeing on a price, confirm whether it's given in Egyptian pounds or a foreign currency. Misunderstandings about the currency can lead to confusion, so it's wise to explain this detail up front.

Bring Small Bills

Having smaller denominations of cash makes the deal smoother. Sellers might claim they don't have change for big bills, so carrying smaller amounts ensures you can pay the agreed-upon price without complications.

CHAPTER 9

9. EXPERIENCING THE NILE

NILE CRUISES: TRADITIONAL FELUCCAS AND LUXURY BOATS

Traditional Feluccas: Authentic and Tranquil

Feluccas are simple, sail-powered wooden boats that have been navigating the Nile for centuries. Their quiet, unhurried nature makes them ideal for travelers who appreciate a peaceful journey. The absence of an engine means that these boats rely on wind and the skill of their captains, offering an intimate experience of the river.

Several operators in Cairo organize felucca rides for short excursions or half-day trips. Companies like Nile Felucca Tours and Felucca Adventures provide well-maintained boats with experienced sailors. Prices for a one-hour ride typically range from $20 to $50, depending on the group size and specific inclusions such as drinks or snacks. These trips often start near Maadi or Zamalek, offering scenic views of Cairo's riverside neighborhoods and the bustling activity along the shore.

Sunset rides are particularly popular, as the fading light casts a golden glow over the river and its surroundings. While feluccas are less about luxury and more about authenticity, their charm lies in the simplicity of the experience. This is a moment to enjoy the river's calm while reflecting on its historical significance.

Luxury Boats: Modern Comforts and Opulent Experiences

Modern cruise boats provide a blend of comfort and style. These vessels are equipped with a range of amenities, including spacious cabins, fine dining, and often entertainment options such as live music or traditional dance performances.

Some of the top companies offering these services include Nile Premium Cruises, Mövenpick Nile Cruise, and Sonesta St. George Nile Cruises. Depending on the package, prices typically range from $150 to $400 per night per person. Multi-day itineraries are also available, providing a chance to journey beyond Cairo to iconic destinations like Luxor and Aswan. However, for those starting their trip in Cairo, shorter packages focus on the highlights of the area, with guided visits to nearby historical sites often included.

The onboard experience is designed for comfort, with air-conditioned spaces, gourmet meals, and panoramic views from deck areas. Evening entertainment may include performances of traditional Egyptian music or belly dancing, adding a cultural dimension to the journey. These cruises balance leisure with exploration, allowing guests to relax while also discovering the rich heritage of the Nile.

Tailored Options for Private and Small Groups

Private tours are available for both feluccas and luxury boats, offering an exclusive way to experience the river. Companies such as Memphis Tours and Nile View Experiences specialize in customized packages, allowing travelers to set their schedules and include special touches like celebratory meals or curated playlists. Prices for private trips vary widely based on the level of customization but generally start at $100 for an hour on a private felucca and upwards of $500 for a private cruise day trip.

These options are ideal for special occasions or for those who prefer a more personalized experience. Many companies also offer packages that include photography services, so travelers can capture their time on the Nile without distraction.

Practical Tips for Booking

When planning a Nile experience, it's important to book with reputable operators to ensure safety and quality. Reviews on platforms like TripAdvisor or direct recommendations from trusted sources can be invaluable. Be sure to check what is included in the price some packages may feature complimentary refreshments, while others might have additional charges for extras.

SUNSET STROLLS ALONG THE CORNICHE

The feeling of strolling along Cairo's Corniche as the sun sets stays with you. Visitors may get a sense of the pace of life in Egypt's vibrant capital as this section of the Nile River's waterfront changes as the day draws to a close. It is a memorable aspect of any trip because of the blend of the dynamic metropolitan atmosphere and the natural beauty.

The Corniche comes alive with bustle as the sky becomes orange, pink, and purple. Street merchants put up their carts with everything from fresh snacks to souvenirs, couples stroll hand in hand, and families congregate to enjoy the refreshing evening breeze. The bustle of the city is more like a background hum in this lively yet serene setting.

The river is perfectly visible from the Corniche, where you may stroll while watching feluccas glide beautifully over the water, their sails reflecting the sunset's hues. It is like witnessing a piece of history as these classic wooden boats glide across the Nile, adding a timeless appeal to the scene.

Many tourists like to sit on the path's low walls to observe the boats and the glistening reflections of city lights as they start to move across the river.

The opportunity to observe how locals spend their evenings is one of the area's pleasures. The Corniche is a place where creativity flourishes, from artists creating portraits to musicians performing upbeat music. It's not uncommon to see a street entertainer enthralling a small group of people or families taking delight in tiny pleasures like laughing together while eating roasted corn that was bought from a local seller.

The stroll is a sensory extravaganza. The subtle scent of the river blends with the smells of freshly baked bread and grilled kebabs from local food vendors. The path is illuminated by streetlights as the sun sets, giving the area a golden glow and producing an almost mystical mood.

The Corniche is about engaging with the city and its residents, not just about taking a stroll. A human touch can be added by stopping to talk with a vendor or observing kids playing by the river. Cairo's people and their tales are where its allure comes to life.

The Corniche provides an opportunity for history buffs to consider how the Nile shaped Egypt's identity. The walk along its banks serves as a reminder of the river's timeless significance, which has been a source of inspiration and life since ancient times.

The lights from buildings and bridges create a glittering display on the lake, making the Corniche vibrant even after the sun has set. The air is filled with laughter and discussion, which makes the atmosphere cozy and welcoming. It's the ideal time to grab a cup of tea at one of the many cafés in the area and watch the city come to life at night.

DINE AND DANCE ON THE RIVER: EVENING ENTERTAINMENT OPTIONS

An evening on a Nile dinner cruise is a must for anybody visiting Cairo. These excursions frequently include an excellent lunch while floating along the river, with views of the city lighted by spectacular lights. The cuisine usually emphasizes Egyptian flavors, with classic meals like koshari, grilled meats, and rich sweets. Guests can sample these culinary delicacies while gliding by prominent sites and taking in the ambiance of the city at night.

Entertainment on these cruises adds a special element to the experience. Traditional music, belly dancing, and Tanoura show a fascinating dance performed by whirling dervishes in colorful costumes are all part of live performances. These artistic exhibits shed light on Egypt's cultural past, providing a compelling spectacle for everyone who watches it.

Cairo also provides smaller, more personal dining experiences along the riverbanks. Many restaurants and events provide outside seating with views of the ocean, often accompanied by mild live music or local bands. This option is great for couples or small groups that wish to spend a quiet evening while yet experiencing the heart of the city.

Certain Cairo establishments combine eating with contemporary entertainment. These venues frequently offer DJs, jazz bands, and even pop concerts, providing a joyful atmosphere ideal for socializing and dancing the night away. The combination of modern and traditional inspirations results in a distinct composition that appeals to a diverse variety of preferences.

Evening entertainment on the Nile isn't restricted to boats and restaurants. Cairo's cultural centers and theaters frequently hold traditional dance and music performances. These performances provide a fantastic opportunity to learn more about the region's traditions. These activities, along with light drinks, offer an enriching alternative to the traditional nightlife.

BIRD WATCHING AND PHOTOGRAPHY OPPORTUNITIES

Popular Locations:

1. Al-Azhar Park

This wide green space is a refuge for bird aficionados, providing a tranquil getaway from the city's busy streets. During migration season, the park's well-kept gardens and trees attract sparrows, warblers, and other unusual visitors. Entrance costs start at around $2 per person. Early mornings are good for observing birds because the park is calmer and the birds are more active.

2. The Giza Pyramids Area.

While the pyramids are well-known for their historical significance, the surrounding area also acts as a resting place for a variety of desert birds. During certain seasons of the year, kestrels and larks can be observed perched on ancient stones or soaring overhead. Access to the pyramids costs roughly $10, but the birdwatching experience is a bonus for guests.

3. Wadi-Degla Protectorate

This protected valley on the outskirts of Cairo provides an undisturbed environment in which birds thrive. The rough environment is home to bee-eaters, hoopoes, and desert wheatears. Entry costs range from $5 to $10. Bringing binoculars and a telephoto lens will improve your experience.

4. Zamalek Island

This green neighborhood, located in the center of Cairo, serves as an unexpected shelter for urban birds. It's quiet streets and green spaces make it a popular place for birdwatching, particularly doves, bulbuls, and egrets. While there is no cost to explore the region, arriving before sunrise or sunset provides the finest light for photography and increases the likelihood of sightings.

Tips for Birdwatching and Photography

1. Select the Right Equipment: When studying birds from a distance, a good pair of binoculars and a camera with a zoom lens may make a huge difference. A solid tripod might also aid in steadying your photographs.

2. Visit Early or Late: Birds are most active in the early morning and shortly before dusk. The illumination at these times is also great for taking beautiful photos.

3. Dress Neutrally: Wearing earth-toned clothing allows you to fit in with the environment and is less likely to disturb the birds.

4. Be Patient: Birds are unpredictable, and they may take some time to appear. Allow yourself to be peaceful and quiet as nature unfolds around you.

5. Respect the Environment: Do not harm the natural habitat. Stay on authorized walkways and avoid making loud noises that will scare the birds away.

Cost breakdown for a day of bird watching in Cairo.

1. Transportation: Depending on your location, transportation services in the city can cost between $5 and $15 to get to birding hotspots.

2. Entry Fees: Expect to pay between $2 and $10 for parks and protectorates.

3. Snacks and Water: Bringing your own is cost-effective, however cafes near some spots may charge $3 to $7 for beverages.

4. Photography Gear: Renting a telephoto lens or camera locally can cost between $20 and $50 per day.

CHAPTER 10

10. PRACTICAL TIPS AND RESOURCES HEALTH AND SAFETY: STAYING HEALTHY IN CAIRO

Hydration is Key

The Egyptian sun can be intense, and temperatures often soar, especially during summer. Staying hydrated is one of the most effective ways to avoid fatigue or heat-related illnesses. Carry a reusable water bottle and refill it frequently with safe drinking water. Bottled water is widely available, and it's advisable to rely on sealed bottles to ensure water quality. Avoid drinking tap water or beverages made with ice from unverified sources, as they may upset your stomach.

Smart Food Choices

Exploring the local cuisine is one of the highlights of any visit to Cairo. From street vendors to high-end restaurants, the city offers a variety of flavors. To minimize the risk of foodborne illness, look for eateries with good hygiene practices and high customer turnover. Avoid consuming raw or undercooked foods, particularly meats and seafood. Freshly prepared dishes served piping hot are often the safest option.

Fruits and vegetables can also be enjoyed if peeled or thoroughly washed with safe water. When in doubt, choose fruits with thick skins that you can remove, such as bananas or oranges. Carrying a small bottle of hand sanitizer or wet wipes can help clean your hands before meals.

Dressing for Comfort and Respect

Cairo's climate and cultural norms should guide your choice of clothing. Lightweight, breathable fabrics can help you stay cool, while long sleeves and pants protect from the sun and insects. Wearing modest attire also shows respect for local customs, especially when visiting religious sites.

When touring the city's historic streets and attractions, comfortable walking shoes are essential. Protect your skin with sunscreen, a hat, and sunglasses to shield yourself from UV rays.

Protecting Your Health

Before traveling, it's wise to visit a healthcare provider to ensure all vaccinations are up to date. Vaccines for Hepatitis A, Typhoid, and Tetanus are often recommended for visitors to Egypt. Carry a small first-aid kit with essentials like adhesive bandages, pain relievers, and any personal medications. Pharmacies are common in Cairo and typically well-stocked, but it's best to be prepared for minor ailments.

To prevent mosquito bites, particularly during the evening, apply a reliable insect repellent and consider using plug-in mosquito repellents in your accommodations. While malaria is not a concern in Cairo, protecting yourself from mosquito-borne illnesses is still a good practice.

Staying Aware of Your Surroundings

Cairo is a dynamic city, and being aware of your surroundings is important. Pay attention to traffic when crossing streets, as the flow can be unpredictable. Stick to well-lit, populated areas when walking after dark, and keep your belongings secure to avoid petty theft.

When using public transportation or hailing a taxi, choose reputable providers. Apps for ride-hailing are a practical and secure way to move around the city. In the event of an emergency, always keep a copy of your passport and travel insurance information on hand.

Managing Air Quality

Cairo can experience episodes of air pollution, which might affect sensitive individuals, such as those with respiratory conditions. To minimize discomfort, monitor air quality levels through local apps or news sources and plan indoor activities during high-pollution periods. If needed, wearing a mask can help filter particulates.

Rest and Recuperation

Exploring Cairo's many attractions can be physically demanding, so it's important to pace yourself. Schedule breaks throughout your day to rest, hydrate, and recharge.

Many cafes and public spaces offer a relaxing environment to sit back and enjoy the moment. Balancing activity with downtime ensures you have the energy to enjoy the city fully.

MONEY MATTERS: CURRENCY, TIPPING, AND BUDGETING

Currency Basics

Cairo uses the Egyptian pound, often abbreviated as EGP or LE. It's a good idea to carry small denominations for daily transactions like buying snacks, and drinks, or paying for transportation. ATMs are widely available, especially in tourist-heavy areas and major hotels, so withdrawing cash isn't a challenge. However, it's best to avoid relying solely on cards since smaller vendors, street markets, and local restaurants often prefer cash.

When exchanging money, it's wise to do so at official banks or authorized currency exchange offices for the best rates. Avoid street exchanges to minimize the risk of scams. Many international visitors also find it useful to carry some U.S. dollars as backup, which can sometimes be accepted in emergencies or easily exchanged for local currency.

Tipping Culture

Tipping is an important part of daily life in Cairo and is appreciated in many situations. Known locally as baksheesh, small tips are customary for services such as carrying luggage, cleaning hotel rooms, or receiving assistance from guides. While tipping isn't mandatory, it's a gesture that shows appreciation for good service.

Leaving around 10% of the bill as a tip is customary, even if a service charge is included. Taxi drivers, on the other hand, do not always expect a tip, but rounding up the fare slightly is a polite way to show gratitude. In places like hotels or organized tours, it's common to tip porters, drivers, and guides a little extra to acknowledge their efforts.

Managing Your Budget

Traveling to Cairo can be as affordable or luxurious as you wish. The cost of living is relatively low compared to Western cities, which means you can experience the city without overspending. To save money, consider staying at mid-range hotels or locally-run guesthouses, which often provide excellent value. Public transportation, such as buses and the metro, is inexpensive, though taxis or ride-hailing apps like Uber offer convenience at slightly higher rates.

Dining at local eateries is not only cost-effective but also a great way to enjoy authentic flavors. Street food like koshary or falafel is delicious and budget-friendly, while upscale restaurants cater to those seeking international or refined dining experiences. Keep track of your spending by allocating daily amounts for food, transportation, and activities, ensuring you don't exceed your travel budget.

Tips for a Smooth Experience

1. Always keep some cash in smaller bills to pay for taxis, tips, and street vendors, as change can be hard to find.

2. Use mobile apps to track exchange rates and stay updated on currency fluctuations.

3. Be cautious about carrying large amounts of cash, and store extra funds securely in a money belt or hotel safe.

APPS AND TOOLS TO ENHANCE YOUR CAIRO EXPERIENCE

Navigating Cairo's Transport System

Cairo's crowded streets can be confusing for newcomers, but ride-hailing applications make the procedure easier. Uber and Careem provide dependable and economical transportation, removing the need to haggle costs or deal with language barriers. These apps also provide an accurate estimate of travel expenditures, providing you peace of mind when budgeting for your trip. They also accept cash or credit card payments, which ensures flexibility.

Apps like Metro Cairo can come in handy for people keen to test Cairo's metro system. This program gives real-time schedule and route changes, allowing you to plan your journeys across the city with ease. It's ideal for traversing the city's huge and reasonably priced subway network.

Exploring local attractions

Apps like Google Maps make it easy to discover Cairo's rich history and culture by providing accurate instructions as well as user reviews and images of major places. Pair this with a guide app like Pocket Egypt, which works offline and includes detailed information about historical sites, museums, and cultural attractions.

GetYourGuide and Viator both provide curated experiences conducted by skilled locals. These applications can help you arrange everything from a personalized guide at the Pyramids to a strolling tour of the Khan el-Khalili bazaar.

Dining and Culinary Experience

Food is an important component of every trip, and apps like TripAdvisor and Zomato make it easy to identify the best places to dine. These systems allow consumers to explore menus, read reviews, and compare ratings to ensure they make an informed decision. Elmenus is a great tool for exploring Cairo's diverse food scene, highlighting hidden gems that would otherwise go undiscovered.

Currency and Budget Management

When handling finances overseas, a trustworthy currency conversion app is crucial. XE Currency offers up-to-date currency rates, allowing you to make educated purchases when shopping or dining. It is very beneficial for understanding costs while working with Egyptian pounds. Budgeting tools like Trail Wallet make it easy to track daily expenses, ensuring you stay within your budget.

Staying connected

While traveling, it is critical to stay in touch with family and friends and have access to important information. Apps like Airalo offer low-cost eSIM solutions, ensuring you always have data for mapping, chatting, and browsing. Alternatively, many local telecom carriers give simple tourist SIM cards, although apps make it easier to set up while on the road.

Language Assistance

While English is widely spoken in tourist destinations, knowing a few Arabic phrases can help make conversations more meaningful. Apps like Google Translate can help overcome language gaps by providing speedy translations and even voice aid during talks. Mondly and Drops are wonderful tools for learning Arabic essentials in a fun and engaging setting.

Travel Safety and Emergency Tools

Safety should always be a top priority, and apps such as bSafe and Red Panic Button provide wonderful piece of mind. These features enable you to share your whereabouts with trusted contacts and issue an alarm if necessary. Cairo is generally a friendly city, but having these services available can make you feel more comfortable throughout your trip.

Capturing memories

Apps such as Snapseed and Lightroom Mobile are ideal for editing images and enhancing trip shots. Pair these with Google Photos for unlimited storage to ensure that every moment is saved. These tools make it simple to create lasting memories of your vacation.

EMERGENCY NUMBERS AND USEFUL CONTACTS

Emergency Services

Cairo's emergency response teams are equipped to handle various situations, from medical emergencies to fire and security issues. These numbers are free to call and accessible 24/7:

Police (for general emergencies): Dial 122

Ambulance services: Dial 123

Fire department: Dial 180

Save these numbers on your phone before your trip, and ensure you have a working mobile connection for quick access. It's also helpful to note your exact location when calling, as clear directions will assist responders in reaching you quickly.

Tourist Police

The Tourist Police are specially trained to assist visitors and are fluent in several languages. They can help with lost items, scams, or general safety concerns. To reach them, dial 126. They're stationed at major tourist sites, airports, and key locations throughout the city, providing a reassuring presence for travelers.

Medical Assistance

Cairo has numerous hospitals and clinics offering excellent care. In case of a medical emergency, contact the nearest hospital or dial 123 for an ambulance. Here are some well-known medical facilities that cater to international travelers:

El Gouna Hospital

International Medical Center

Dar Al Fouad Hospital

Bring along any personal drugs you might need for the trip, along with a basic first-aid kit. For minor illnesses or pharmacy needs, you'll find many 24-hour pharmacies in the city with English-speaking staff.

Your Embassy

In unforeseen circumstances, your country's embassy can be an invaluable resource. Whether you need help replacing a lost passport, legal assistance, or simply advice, having their contact details on hand is critical. Major embassies in Cairo include:

United States Embassy: +20 2 2797 3300

United Kingdom Embassy: +20 2 2791 6000

Canadian Embassy: +20 2 2461 2200

Check your embassy's website for additional services and advice specific to travelers from your country.

Transportation and Road Assistance

Getting around Cairo can be an adventure in itself, but should you encounter any issues, it's good to know who to call:

Traffic Police: Dial 128

Roadside Assistance: Contact your rental car agency or use local services like Egypt Auto Assistance.

For public transportation concerns, including taxis and metro services, most operators are accommodating and will help direct you to the appropriate contacts.

Local Helplines and Information

Apart from emergency services, several helplines and services in Cairo are designed to support travelers:

Tourist Information: Dial 19654 for updates on attractions, events, and local tips.

Electricity or Gas Issues: Dial 121 for electricity or 129 for gas services in case of an emergency in your accommodations.

Directory Assistance: Dial 140 for phone number inquiries.

INSIDER TIPS FOR AVOIDING TOURIST TRAPS

Research Before You Arrive

Understanding the city's layout and cultural norms can save you from unnecessary expenses. Before you head out, read about the places you plan to visit, including the Great Pyramids of Giza, Khan el-Khalili Bazaar, and the Egyptian Museum. While these spots are worth exploring, being well-informed about entrance fees, operational hours, and transportation options will help you avoid being overcharged or misled by unofficial guides.

Use Trusted Transportation

Cairo's bustling streets are teeming with taxis, but not all of them operate on metered systems. To avoid inflated fares, rely on ride-hailing apps or insist on using a metered taxi before the journey begins. If public transportation feels like an adventure you're ready to take on, familiarize yourself with the metro system it's affordable, efficient, and a glimpse into everyday life in the city.

Be Cautious with Guides and Tours

Unlicensed guides often approach tourists near major attractions, offering seemingly great deals for private tours. While tempting, these tours may lack authenticity or cover only a limited scope of the site. Instead, book through reputable tour operators or seek recommendations from your hotel. Many official guides are knowledgeable and add real value to your visit.

Negotiate Smartly When Shopping

Markets in Cairo are a sensory delight, but bargaining is part of the culture. Vendors may quote higher prices initially, expecting you to negotiate. While this is normal, avoid becoming too focused on getting the lowest price; instead, aim for a fair deal both parties can agree on. Stay polite and firm, and be prepared to walk away if the price doesn't suit you.

Avoid Overpaying for Food and Drinks

While the food scene in Cairo offers delicious and affordable options, restaurants near major tourist hubs often charge premium prices. For a more authentic and reasonably priced meal, explore eateries frequented by locals. When dining out, ask about service charges and taxes to avoid surprises on your bill.

Be Mindful of Touts

It's common for individuals to approach tourists offering camel rides, photo opportunities, or souvenirs, often at inflated prices. Politely decline if you're not interested, and avoid making eye contact or engaging in conversation to reduce pressure. If you do choose to participate, always agree on a price upfront to prevent last-minute disagreements.

Choose Your Souvenirs Wisely

While the allure of bringing back a piece of Cairo is undeniable, some shops sell counterfeit or overpriced items claiming to be authentic artifacts. Stick to government-certified shops or bazaars known for quality craftsmanship. Look for items like handmade jewelry, textiles, or traditional spices that reflect the city's culture and heritage.

Stay Aware of Entrance Fees

Many attractions in Cairo have separate pricing tiers for locals and tourists. This is standard practice in many countries but can lead to confusion if you're unaware. Always confirm the price at the ticket counter and carry small bills to avoid overpaying due to lack of change.

Trust but Verify Information

Well-meaning strangers may offer unsolicited advice or directions, sometimes leading you to shops or services where they receive a commission. While friendliness is a hallmark of Egyptian hospitality, it's best to double-check recommendations with a trusted source, such as your hotel concierge or a verified travel guide.

Enjoy Cairo Like a Local

One of the best ways to experience Cairo authentically is to observe and learn from the locals. Visit less-touristy neighborhoods, try street food, and take time to absorb the rhythm of everyday life. These moments often leave the deepest impressions and cost far less than overly curated tourist experiences.

CHAPTER 11

APPENDICES

SUGGESTED ITINERARIES: 2-DAY, 5-DAY, AND 7-DAY PLANS

2-Day Itinerary: The Essentials

Day 1: Start your journey with a visit to the world-famous Giza Pyramids. Spend your morning marveling at these ancient wonders and the Great Sphinx. A camel ride can add a bit of adventure to your exploration. After lunch at a nearby restaurant, head to the Egyptian Museum in Tahrir Square. The museum houses an incredible collection of artifacts, including treasures from King Tutankhamun's tomb. Wrap up your day with a relaxing dinner aboard a Nile River cruise.

Day 2: Begin the day in Islamic Cairo with a visit to the Citadel of Saladin. Explore the Mosque of Muhammad Ali and enjoy panoramic views of the city. Next, head to the historic Khan El Khalili Bazaar, where you can wander through its narrow alleys, shop for unique souvenirs, and savor traditional Egyptian coffee. Take a stroll through Al-Azhar Park, a verdant haven in the center of Cairo, to cap off your journey.

5-Day Itinerary: A Deeper Dive into Cairo

Day 1 & 2: Follow the 2-day plan to cover the must-see sights of Giza, the Egyptian Museum, the Citadel, and Khan El Khalili.

Day 3: Dedicate this day to exploring Coptic Cairo. Visit the Hanging Church, one of the oldest churches in the city, and the Coptic Museum to learn about the history of Christianity in Egypt. Don't miss the Ben Ezra Synagogue, steeped in religious and cultural significance. Later, take a stroll along the Maadi Corniche, a quieter area by the Nile.

Day 4: Experience the modern side of Cairo with a visit to Zamalek, a trendy district known for its art galleries, boutiques, and cafes. Spend the afternoon at the Museum of Islamic Art, which boasts one of the world's most comprehensive collections of Islamic artifacts. End your day with a sunset view from the Cairo Tower.

Day 5: Head to Saqqara to explore the Step Pyramid of Djoser and the nearby Dahshur pyramids, including the unique Bent Pyramid. These sites offer a quieter alternative to Giza and an opportunity to delve further into Egypt's ancient history.

7-Day Itinerary: The Complete Cairo Experience

Day 1 to 5: Begin with the 5-day plan to cover Cairo's historical, cultural, and modern highlights.

Day 6: Take a day trip to Fayoum, a nearby city rich in natural beauty and archaeological sites. Explore the stunning Lake Qarun, the Wadi El Rayan waterfalls, and the ancient ruins of Karanis. If you have time, stop by the UNESCO-listed Wadi Al-Hitan, also known as the Valley of Whales, for a glimpse into Egypt's prehistoric past.

Day 7: Spend your final day soaking up Cairo's vibrant atmosphere. Visit the Abdeen Palace Museum to learn about Egypt's modern history or take a food tour to taste the local cuisine. As the evening sets in, return to the Nile for one last serene moment in this bustling metropolis.

KEY PHRASES IN EGYPTIAN ARABIC: COMMUNICATING WITH LOCALS

Greetings and Politeness

In Egyptian culture, greetings are an important way of showing respect. Start with "Salaam Alaikum" (peace be upon you) as a friendly hello. The common response is "Wa Alaikum Salaam" (and peace be upon you). For casual settings, a simple "Sabah El Kheir" (good morning) or "Masa El Kheir" (good evening) works well, with the response being "Sabah El Nour" or "Masa El Nour" (morning or evening of light).

Adding phrases like "Shukran" (thank you) and "Afwan" (you're welcome) to your vocabulary can go a long way. Egyptians appreciate politeness, and these words will help you navigate day-to-day interactions smoothly.

Asking for Directions

Navigating Cairo's lively streets can be a challenge, but locals are usually happy to help. Phrases such as "Fein..." (where is...) can be followed by your destination, like "Fein el metro?" (where is the metro?). If you need clarification, you can ask, "Momken te'ool tany?" (can you say it again?).

When pointing to something on a map or your phone, the word "Hena" (here) is useful, while "Hodoorak" (you, for a man) or "Hodorek" (you, for a woman) can politely direct the conversation.

Shopping and Bargaining

Cairo's markets are legendary, and a few phrases will help you navigate the art of bargaining. Start with "Bekam?" (how much?) to ask the price. If the amount seems high, you can say "Ghali awi" (too expensive). A friendly "Momken takhfeed?" (can you lower the price?) often leads to negotiation.

Ending the conversation with "Shukran gazilan" (thank you very much) leaves a positive impression, even if you don't make a purchase.

Dining and Eating Out

Ordering food in a local restaurant can be a delightful experience when you know a few key phrases. "Ana ayiz..." (I want...) for men or "Ana ayza..." for women can be followed by the dish you'd like to order. For example, "Ana ayiz koshary" (I want koshary). If you're unsure about a dish, "Dah eih?" (what is this?) will help you learn more.

When asking for water, say "Mayya law samaht" (water, please), and when the meal is over, ask for the check with "El hesab, law samaht" (the bill, please).

Expressing Yourself

Sometimes, expressing how you feel can be important. If you're too hot, you can say "Ana haran" (I'm hot) or "Ana bardan" (I'm cold). If you don't understand something, a polite "Ana mish fahim" (I don't understand) for men or "Ana mish fahma" for women can clear up confusion.

Making Friends

Egyptians are known for their hospitality, and engaging in small talk can lead to meaningful connections. Compliments like "Gameel" (beautiful) or "Shater" (well done) are great conversation starters. Asking "Enta/Ana min fein?" (where are you from?) can bridge the gap between you and the locals.

CAIRO FOR FAMILIES: KID-FRIENDLY ACTIVITIES AND TIPS

Engaging Historical Explorations

The pyramids of Giza and the Great Sphinx are must-see attractions for both children and adults. Families may experience the magic of these ancient wonders through stories about pharaohs and buried treasures, which bring history to life for inquiring minds. Consider taking a camel or horse carriage trip around the area to offer another layer of pleasure for the kids.

To complement the outdoor excursion, the Egyptian Museum houses an outstanding collection of artifacts, including Tutankhamun's riches. The museum's exhibits pique youngsters' interest, allowing them to learn intriguing stories about ancient Egypt in an interactive atmosphere. To make the visit more interesting, search for tours developed with children in mind, which include simplified explanations and exciting activities.

Outdoor Fun and Nature Escapes

Cairo's parks and gardens are ideal for families seeking green space. Al-Azhar Park, a wonderfully planned urban oasis, has wide spaces for children to play and stunning vistas for parents to enjoy. Families can picnic, hire bikes, or simply rest under the shade of trees. The park's family-friendly ambiance makes it an ideal place to relax after experiencing the bustling metropolis.

The Giza Zoo is another popular destination for younger people. The zoo, which houses a range of animals, offers children the opportunity to learn about wildlife in a dynamic setting. Parents might organize a half-day trip here to let their children explore and engage with nature.

Hands-on learning experiences

Consider going to KidZania Cairo, an innovative edutainment center where kids can role-play various occupations in a pleasant, controlled environment. From pilot to chef, the possibilities for imaginative play are limitless, making it popular with children of all ages.

The Planetarium Science Center of the Bibliotheca Alexandrina is ideal for science enthusiasts. While slightly outside Cairo, it is well worth the drive for its interactive exhibits and fascinating shows that expose children to the mysteries of science and astronomy.

Family-Friendly Dining Options

Dining in Cairo is a joy for families, with many restaurants offering child-friendly menus. Many restaurants combine wonderful native flavors with worldwide favorites, ensuring that even picky eaters find something to like. Seek for settings with play areas or outside seats to keep the kids entertained while parents enjoy their dinner.

Practical Tips for a Smooth Trip

1. Plan: Cairo can be overwhelming for first-time visitors, so create an itinerary that mixes sightseeing and rest. Include a variety of indoor and outdoor activities to account for changing weather or energy levels.

2. Stay Hydrated: The city's environment can be heated, so bring lots of water and take frequent rests to avoid weariness.

3. Transportation: While taxis and ride-sharing apps are helpful for families, hiring private tours for longer journeys can assure a hassle-free experience.

CONCLUSION

As we conclude this book, it is evident that Cairo is more than just a destination; it is an experience, a fusion of history, culture, and modern vibrancy. Throughout this book, we've wandered through the bustling alleys of Khan El Khalili, stood in the shadow of Giza's great Pyramids, and visited the serene gardens of Al-Azhar Park. Each destination was carefully chosen to enhance your stay, combining profound historical knowledge with practical travel advice to make your Cairo journey both educational and entertaining.

From trying classic Egyptian foods like koshari and ful medames to seeing a play at the Cairo Opera House, the activities we've described offer a complete look into Egypt's capital's past and present. Whether you've been attracted by comprehensive descriptions of Cairo's world-class museums or the lovely evenings spent boating the Nile, Cairo has something for everyone.

With 2025 approaching, now is the ideal time to plan your visit to Cairo. The city is always growing, with new attractions and upgraded amenities guaranteeing that each visit is as exciting as the last. Whether you're a seasoned traveler returning to favorite haunts or a first-timer eager to discover every nook, Cairo delivers memories to last a lifetime.

So what are you waiting for? Book your trip to Cairo now and experience the heart of Egypt for yourself. Enjoy the journey, explore the rich fabric of history, and let Cairo's dynamic energy inspire your next great travel tale.

Made in United States
Troutdale, OR
12/30/2024

27420644R00110